CHINA
IN A CHANGING
WORLD

Gar Pardy

Agora Books™
Ottawa, Canada

China in a Changing World

Copyright © 2020 by Gar Pardy

All Rights Reserved. No part of this book may be reproduced, stored in a retrieval system, or transmitted, in any form or by any means, electronic, mechanical, photocopying, recording or otherwise, without the expressed written consent of Agora Books.

The views, opinions and perceptions of the author of the book herein expressed in this text are intended to support civil and creative social discussion in Canada and internationally.

Care has been taken to trace the ownership/source of any references made in this text. The publisher welcomes any information that will enable a rectification in subsequent edition(s) of any incorrect or omitted reference or credit.

Agora Books
B.P. 24191
300 Eagleson Rd.
Kanata, Ontario K2M 2C3 CANADA

Agora Books is a trade mark of The Agora Cosmopolitan which is a not-for-profit corporation.

ISBN 978-1-927538-61-6

Book cover artwork is by Antonella.

For Laurel, Julian, and Michael, Kari and Rowan. *Close travellers yesterday, today, and tomorrow.*

Table of Contents

Preface 7
1. Exordium, Digest, and Culminations 9
2. The Global Stage – the Power of Power. 31
3. Beginnings – Comings and Goings of Empires. 36
4. Back to China and When Today Started. 43
5. Lots of Borders – Some Compromises but No Need to Fight 45
6. Beyond Asia 63
7. External Wars and Internal Conflicts 76
8. Stormy Seas. 85
9. Banks – More Than Money. 93
10. Regional Organizations – Collective Comfort for the Neighbours 97
11. Stumbling Americans and Wandering Russians – Recovery or Decay. 101
12. Comings and Goings in Global Power Relationships. 107
13. Canada and China – Problems but No Solutions 129
14. A New World – Conclusions and an Agenda for the Future 142
About the author 153

Preface

This book rose out of an effort to analyse how Canada could resolve the inter-related problems of the United States' request for the extradition of Meng Wanzhou and the release of Canadians Michael Kovrig and Michael Spavor following their arbitrary detentions, arrests, and indictments in China. With the luxury of abundant time created by the arrival of the coronavirus pandemic along the shores of the Rideau, Ottawa, and Gatineau rivers, I was motivated to examine the role of an ascendant China in a changing world. I hope this examination will assist in the early return of Kovrig and Spavor to Canada. Moreover, the book provides ideas for how the world might adjust and adapt to a China that is influential and involved in most current global issues, and discusses the role of other influential countries, including the United States, Russia, India, and the European Union, as Chinese involvement and influence grows. For this, I consulted with retired colleagues, who, in the tradition of diplomacy, remain nameless—all mistakes are my own. The validity of my conclusions will be revealed as the future unfolds.

1. Exordium, Digest, and Culminations

China's long-term strategic objective is to eliminate the United States Armed Forces from its contiguous seas and terminate its role as the security guarantor for the countries of the region, especially Taiwan. In a perverse way, the policies of the United States have given indirect and direct encouragement, if not support, to the objectives of China. It has undermined its own reliability as a guarantor of security for countries of the region.

****

In the seventy-five years since the Second World War, global progress has been extraordinary. Even in the middle of a global pandemic, we live knowing there is a global will to face that problem of nature. We also have the knowledge and experience to face a host of other problems associated with the fertility and sterility of the human mind. Central to this progress is the continuation and enhancement of the globalization of "will."

Globalization, in the minds of some, is the source of many of today's ills and problems. They hark back to a badly remembered past as if there are answers for the future in its death and destruction. The millions who died in the Second World War, ending as it did with the cataclysmic introduction of the ultimate force of nature, the atomic bomb, have faded from our collective memories. In a moment of deep self-reflection, J. Robert Oppenheimer, one of the "fathers of the atomic bomb," reached back to Hindu texts to graphically describe what was then underway: "Now I am become Death, the destroyer of worlds."

Equally, as knowledge of the millions of deaths within the extermination camps of Nazism emerged after the war, there was collective horror and shame. In reaction, there was an understanding that collective effort was needed to offer redress for the 2,500-year-old Jewish diaspora. The creation of the state of Israel, in large part by the collective will of the Jewish people in 1948 and its legitimization by the newly created United Nations, provided that redress. In doing so, it destroyed and created again the collective will of the Palestinians.

In a perverse way, the use of nuclear weapons and collective redress for the millions of Jewish, Romani, and other peoples murdered in the Second World War gave rise to the construction of a new world. These events of mass horror were accompanied by the unity of most of the world's independent nations. Within the Allied effort to defeat the Axis countries, the initiating step to build this new world was taken. This was the true globalization.

Today there is an urgent need for unity among the countries of the world. The large successes of the past seventy-five years have in turn created new problems, little anticipated when our international institutions were created as the Second World War came to an end. But the creation of those institutions carries instructions for us today in any effort to organize the collective international will needed for the coming decades. As such, an appropriate starting point is an examination of the conditions and the efforts made in establishing those institutions not so many years ago. In the midst of a global pandemic, they provide an example of a unity of purpose and vision for us in today's troubled world.

The Creation of the Post-War World

As early as December 1941, following the Japanese attack on Pearl Harbour and the formal entry of the United States into the war in Europe, Allied countries met in Washington, D.C., in the Arcadia

Conference. Apart from the agreement by the United States and Britain on military strategy in Europe, North Africa, and the Pacific, the Arcadia Conference issued the joint *Declaration by United Nations*, drafted by the Americans, which became the foundation for the United Nations organization today. Twenty-six attending countries, including Canada, China, and the USSR, signed the declaration on January 1, 1942. In doing so, they pledged adherence to the August 1941 Atlantic Charter (with the addition of a freedom of religion provision), declared full support for the war effort, and pledged not to make a separate armistice or peace with the Axis powers. By 1945, twenty-one other states had signed the declaration, representing the vast majority of the then-independent states.

Less than two years after the Arcadia Conference in late August 1943, the foreign ministers of the United States, the United Kingdom, the Soviet Union, and China met in Moscow and further recognized the establishment of an international organization dedicated to international peace and security and based on the sovereign equality of all states.

A year later, between August 21 and October 7, 1944, the Dumbarton Oaks Conference, again in Washington, D.C., gave greater specificity to the new international organization. In *Proposals for the Establishment of a General International Organization*, the United States, the Soviet Union, the United Kingdom, and China agreed that the new organization would include three bodies: a General Assembly of all members; a Security Council of eleven members, five of which would be permanent; and an International Court of Justice. Responsibility for the prevention of future wars would reside with the Security Council. The *Proposals* also included the requirement for member states to provide armed forces in support of Security Council decisions on wars and acts of aggression.

Four months later on February 11, 1945, at Yalta on the Crimean Peninsula in the Soviet Union, the same four foreign ministers agreed they would have a veto power in the Security Council's decision making. The same meeting also called for the United Nations Conference on International Organization to meet. In less than two months, on April 25, 1945, the conference opened in San Francisco. Fifty countries attended and while there was minor difficulty around membership, the conference agreed to the Dumbarton Oaks *Proposals* and in turn issued the *Charter of the United Nations* on June 25, 1945. Four months later on October 26, 1945, the charter came into effect, having being signed by the United States, the Soviet Union, the United Kingdom, China, and newly liberated France as the fifth permanent member of the Security Council, along with the majority of the other signatory countries.

Completing this intense period of collective international action in institution-building, financial experts from forty-four countries met at Bretton Woods in New Hampshire in July 1944 for the United Nations Monetary and Financial Conference. This was in the immediate aftermath of the Normandy landings and even with that large preoccupation, in only three weeks, the delegates established a system of rules and institutions governing the international monetary system. The system required countries to maintain external monetary exchange rates by using an established price for gold. John Maynard Keynes, the most influential economist of the twentieth century, represented Britain at the conference and was in opposition to the continued use of gold as the basis for the new system.

However, Harry White, the head of the American delegation and an economist little-known outside of Washington, insisted on its continued use, reflecting the existing importance of gold and the huge stockpile available to the United States. Twenty-five years later, Keynes proved to be right when the United States dropped the connection of the American dollar to the price of gold. Today, gold still glitters for millions, but only in the dreams of those needing a tangible edge against the future. Gold now sells at over US$2,000 per ounce; it was selling in the mid-$30s when Keynes and White had their discussions in 1944.

The monetary aspects of the agreement lasted only until August 1971, when the United States unilaterally terminated the involvement of the American dollar in the arrangement. But the institutional arrangements established with the Bretton Woods agreement—namely, the International Monetary Fund (IMF) and the International Bank for Reconstruction and Development (IBRD)—live on and continue to provide the world with high-level management and cooperation on many economic and monetary matters.

China in a Changing World

The IBRD is now part of the World Bank group along with four additional components: The International Development Association (IDA), the International Finance Corporation (IFC), the Multilateral Investment Guarantee Agency (MIGA), and the International Centre for Settlement of Investment Disputes (ICSID).

This cooperation by a wide variety of countries, at a time when they were preoccupied in fighting a global war, is worthy of recall and remembrance. The countries involved understood and accepted that the world emerging from the war would be a different one than the world that entered the war. Also, there was a common understanding of the enormous mistakes made by the "victors" in the aftermath of the First World War, which had created the conditions for the war they were now fighting. When delegates from thirty-two countries met at the Paris Peace Conference in Versailles in 1919–1920, they were intent on punishing the losers and awarding the spoils of war to the victors. The resulting treaties were collectively based on the understanding that "Germany and her allies" carried total responsibility for the war and had to forfeit their overseas colonies and pay enormous reparations.

Before the end of the Second World War, the Allied countries, largely led by the United States and the United Kingdom, with the cooperation of the Soviet Union and the involvement of China, decided the post-war world needed new global institutions of collective management and assiduously engaged in their creation. From the Arcadia Conference in December 1941 to the San Francisco Conference in April 1945, U.S. President Franklin D. Roosevelt provided constant and inspired leadership to this effect. Roosevelt died on April 12, 1945, just as the San Francisco Conference was beginning, but his intent on the new world order was carried forward to its conclusion by his successor, Harry S. Truman, with the first meeting of the United Nations General Assembly in London on January 10, 1946. Fifty-one countries attended the meeting, and the second meeting was held in New York City on October 23, 1946. Two years ago, in 2018, South Sudan became its 193rd member, and there will still be a few more to come. This is the true reflection of globalization.

Canada was an active participant in these meetings leading to the creation of the United Nations. Its large military role in the war, along with an economy among the strongest in the world, gave it an importance and influence at the San Francisco Conference that has faded in relative terms over the years. The failure of Canada's two recent attempts for membership in the Security Council reflects that fading, and it equally reflects the success of the United Nations as reflective of a much larger and complex world seeking influence on the predations of the global powers. In San Francisco in 1945, Canada sought to give voice to this large majority of "middle powers." As Barry Steers wrote in *Policy Options* on September 1, 2005, "what really mattered was the need on the one hand to trim the presumptions and the privileges of the great powers (even if the political realities meant that this could be done only at the margins), and on the other to head off the more legalistic organizational principle reflected in the doctrine of state equality (which for obvious reasons enjoyed a certain popularity among some of the smaller players)."

Canadian Prime Minister Justin Trudeau reflected this in his statement on June 26, 2020, celebrating the United Nations' seventy-fifth anniversary: "As a proud founding member of the UN, Canada continues to play a productive and collaborative role at the UN and on the international stage. [...] We believe that real change is possible if we continue to engage with international partners to reach these goals—together." He went on to say that "On this day, let us reflect on the indispensable role of the UN in bringing the international community together, and recommit to our values of peace, justice, human dignity, inclusion, and cooperation as we continue on our path toward a better world for everyone."

"A better world for everyone" remains the goal today just as it was back in the last days of the Second World War. In those intervening seventy-five years, the wisdom and forethought of those involved in the creation of the new institutions have stood the test of time. But just as in 1945, today the world's countries must face the consequences of that earlier success, along with new ones that have emerged and that dominate our daily lives.

First and foremost is the need to recognize for the first time in history that there is today an inclusivity of all people. The instrument of that inclusivity is the "state" in legal terms, but the "country" in our daily conversations. Only fifty-one states attended the first meeting of the General Assembly of the United Nations in London in October 1945. Today, 193 states attend the Assembly meetings. South Sudan was the last to become a member when, in 2018, it emerged from a decades-long civil war with Sudan. This war was based on race, religion, and regionality, and not surprisingly, in the aftermath of South Sudan's independence, the same issues now dominate the newly independent state. These same factors significantly impact other countries as well, some of which have attained independence in recent years, and others where tensions of race, religion, and regionality have yet to be resolved.

The world's organization in 1945 was based on the predations of European countries, which, during the sixteenth and seventeenth centuries, pushed against the boundaries of their "known" world and came to dominate the lives of billions in their newly "discovered" lands. These European countries, including Holland, Portugal, Spain, France, England, Belgium, Germany, and Italy, established an age of imperialism and colonialism. In the late nineteenth and early twentieth centuries, these European countries were joined by Russia, the United States, and Japan in the expansion of their dominions to other parts of the world. Turkey, before it became Turkey and was known as the Ottoman Empire, was a precursor to this process, as its domination extended from the northwest corner of Africa into the lands of the Balkans and central Asia. The countries involved called this period the Age of Discovery, or in some cases, the Age of Conquest, and, harkening back to earlier times in human history, referred to the conquered lands as parts of their empires. This Age of "Discovery" and domination was legitimized by politicians, pundits, preachers, and poets.

Wars between and among these imperial and colonizing countries led to the collapse of their worldwide system of domination. The wars of the first half of the twentieth century, involving all of the colonizing countries, created the conditions that undermined and destroyed their relationships with the overseas elements of their empires. Associated with that "undermining" in the aftermath of the First World War was the historical urge to punish the losers. And for the most part, there were always losers. The victors who emerged from the Second World War provided a more understanding approach and the losers were provided with the conditions for a successful future.

Historically, China did not take advantage of its successful ventures into the larger world, nor did they stay for long. In the early thirteenth century, Genghis Khan united the nomadic peoples of Northeast Asia, and in turn, led his armies out of what is now northern China into southern China, Central Asia, Europe, and parts of the Middle East. Many of his troops and generals over time included non-Mongols, all willing cooperants in the creation of the Mongol Empire. It was the largest empire of contiguous territory in the history of the world, equal to or larger than the Soviet Empire of the twentieth century. This was a murderous period, with millions killed throughout the conquered lands. At the same time, the predations of Genghis Khan and his heirs expanded the Silk Road and the extensive land trade route into Europe for commerce from what is today mainland China.

Early in the second half of the fourteenth century, family disputes among the descendants of Genghis Khan—the Yuan Dynasty—led to the disintegration of Mongol domination of China. In turn, the Ming Dynasty emerged in 1368 and ruled most of what is modern-day China. Today, Mongols are one of over fifty ethnic minorities in the country, making up less than 6 percent of the people of China. They are largely concentrated in Inner Mongolia, and represent twice the number of Mongols in the neighbouring state of Mongolia. *Sic transit Gloria.*

In less than fifty years, early in the Ming Dynasty, another person from Asia reached into the lands of the western Indian Ocean. In a series of seven voyages between 1405 and 1433, exploring mariner Zheng He commanded a flotilla of hundreds of ships—not of conquest, but of taxation, collecting tributary payments from lands in the Indian Ocean world. In part, he was seeking to demonstrate Chinese control over the maritime trade routes into the Middle East, which were expanded during the Mongol Empire established by Genghis Khan during his land invasions. Problems in China preoccupied the Ming emperor and despite the success of Zheng's voyages, Zheng was ordered by the emperor to cease his efforts, and most of his ships were subsequently destroyed. His ships were four to five times larger than anything then being built in Europe.

China in a Changing World

In the six hundred years after the voyages of Zheng He, China had little impact on the external world except for the hundreds of thousands of people who left and established new lives and homes around the world. In some cases, these Chinese diasporic communities were culturally and economically large, and sometimes politically significant as well. During this same period, Europe's colonizing powers reached into China and forced the acceptance of their presence onto weakened and weakening emperors. This period gave rise to the forces of change and revolution in China that became manifest with the 1949 establishment of a government ruled by the Chinese Communist Party. This period of "shame" still influences China's policy towards the world today.

The global nature of the Second World War required significant improvements in the supporting tools of war. This was most evident with the airplane and long-distance communications. Before the Second World War, transoceanic air travel was for adventurers. Over the Atlantic Ocean, 50 percent of these early flights ended in watery graves. The introduction of the water-based Clipper aircraft (the C-314) by the Boeing Aircraft Company provided a sound basis for all transoceanic air travel. The design of this 1938 aircraft was influenced by the need to meet the 2,500-mile distance between California and Hawaii, and was easily adapted to meet fast transoceanic travel throughout the world. On the other hand, German technology centred on the dirigible ended with the 1937 fiery crash of the *Hindenburg* on the outskirts of New York City.

Even before the war started, the principles associated with the jet engine were experimented with in Britain, the United States, and Germany. These principles found origins in thirteenth-century Chinese rocketry, which used gunpowder for fireworks and weaponry. War bred the impulse for jet-powered aircraft and before WWII ended, both Germany with the Messerschmitt Me 262 and Britain with the Gloster Meteor had entered service in 1944. The postwar period saw jet engine technology carried into commercial air travel with the ill-fated British de Havilland Comet, the French Sud Aviation Caravelle, and the Russian Tupolev Tu-104 aircraft. But it was the creation of the American Boeing 707 in 1957 and the Douglas DC-8 in 1959 that formed the basis for all long-range air travel thereafter. These two aircraft and their numerous successors shortened worldwide travel to less than twenty-four hours.

Tactical and longer-range communications during the First World War were rudimentary. Tactical communications still used horses, bicycles, motorcycles, and men on foot. Global communications were tied to shortwave radio using the Marconi code, but in time, there were underwater cables and Marconi-based wired systems for data and later for voice. Matters had not improved appreciably by the start of the Second World War, but again, the global nature of that war laid the basis for the systems of the future we use today. The introduction of various land-based technical systems and equipment and the launch of communications satellites combined to make international communications as available to the wanderer in the Sahara as they are in downtown St. John's, Newfoundland.

These two complementary technologies, the jet aircraft and satellite communications, provide the technical foundation for today's world. In doing so, they act as the foundation for the effort needed to revalidate and provide additional mandates and resources to the international institutions constructed during and after the Second World War. In some instances, it is necessary to identify and construct the new ones needed to meet our current needs.

As discussed above, the fifty-one countries that came together in 1946 for the first meeting of the United Nations General Assembly in London were largely allies in the war against Nazism, fascism, and Japanese expansionism. Their coherence in creating the institutions for the postwar world did not remain much longer than the first meetings. Countries dominated by European and American imperial and colonial systems were liberated by the war as much as were the countries dominated by Nazism, fascism, and the Japanese. Even as the Pacific War ended with the use of atomic bombs over Hiroshima and Nagasaki on August 6 and 9, 1945, Indonesians declared their independence from Dutch rule on August 17, 1945. It took the Dutch until 1949 to acknowledge the reality of that declaration. The United States granted independence to the Philippines, symbolically, on July 4, 1946. The idea of sovereignty was firmly established and became the force that created today's United Nations, where 193 countries collectively ponder the world's future.

China in a Changing World

The British, near bankruptcy after the war, were not long in accepting this new reality, and in 1947 agreed to depart the "Jewel in the Crown" of its empire in South Asia. India, Pakistan, Sri Lanka, and Burma were not long in taking responsibility for their own affairs and involvement in the new world. Even in the North Atlantic, the newly elected Labour government in London decided that it was time to cut its responsibility for the island of Newfoundland. Through backroom deals with Ottawa and still-questionable referenda, the island became part of Canada in 1949. In doing so, Canada did become a country that was from sea to sea to sea and Newfoundlanders gained a new and better future. For many, the British Empire ended when Hong Kong became a Special Administrative Region of China on July 1, 1997. Today, Beijing has destroyed the idea that Hong Kong partially exists in a world beyond its control. The last bit of historical "unequal treaties" has been eliminated.

The French, Spanish, and Portuguese took much longer in accepting the reality of this emerging new world and to depart, along with settlers from their colonies in Africa, Asia, and the Caribbean. In France, it took the formation of a new republic (the fifth since Napoleon died alone on a small island in the South Atlantic in 1821), and it took the death of long-time fascist leaders in Spain and Portugal before their iron fists were loosened from colonized lands in Africa and Asia.

The Wars to End Wars

As the First World War was starting its march to massive death, destruction, and decay, novelist H. G. Wells described it in August 1914 as "the war that will end war." Over time, this phrase, with slight variations, became the sardonic descriptor of the First World War and remains in use today. It was a wiser group of leaders involved in 1945 and there was little interest in trying to deceive a global public that the war just ending had anything to do with ending war. Rather, there was an understanding that war, as with most human endeavours, was in one guise or another a constant feature of the relationships among peoples and states, and within states. The construction of these leaders of the United Nations and the magnanimity of postwar relations with the defeated countries were directed towards creating the conditions where war could be constrained, restrained, and even, possibly, removed.

The First and Second World Wars established the ignoble standard for deaths in such conflicts. Even with the passage of years since there is no complete accounting, but the available numbers are worth highlighting. In the First World War, there were some sixteen to forty million violent deaths; in the Second World War, the estimate ranges from fifty-six million to eighty-five million. Some twenty to twenty-five million people died in the Second Sino-Japanese War between 1936 and 1939. However, since 1945, there is evidence supporting the statements that (a) wars between states have sharply reduced; (b) the number of intrastate wars has increased significantly; and (c) non-state actors in wars have come to dominate. One significant development of post-1945 conflicts is that the number of resulting deaths has decreased significantly from when wars were predominately inter-state.

The enumeration of these conflicts is relatively easy; it is much more difficult to determine accurately the associated number of deaths. Even with the overall decline in such deaths since 1945, there are worrisome indications the number of deaths in the past decade has increased. To illustrate this, below is a selected list of wars, participants, and associated violent deaths since the Second World War.

- France–Indochina War 1946–1954 400,00
- Greek Civil War 1946–1949 158,000
- India–Pakistan Kashmir Conflict 1947–present 80,000–110,000
- Colombia La Violencia 1948–1958 192,000–250,000
- Arab–Israeli Wars 1946–present 116,074 +
- Korean War 1950–1953 1.5–4.5 million
- France–Algeria War 1954–1962 400,000–1.5 million
- Vietnam War 1955–1975 2.4–4.3 million
- Sudan Civil War 1955–1972 500,000 +
- Nigerian Civil War 1967–1970 1–3 million

- India–Pakistan Bangladesh 1971   3 million
- Afghanistan War   1978–present   1.2–2 million
- Soviet–Afghan War   1979–1989   600,000–2 million
- Iran–Iraq War   1980–1988   289,000–1.1 million

And over the last two decades, there have been the following wars:

- American–Afghan War   2001–present   47,000–62,000
- Iraq War   2003–2011   405,000–654,965
- War in Darfur   2003–present   300,000 +
- Kivu, Congo Conflict   2004–present   100,000 +
- War in Northwest Pakistan 2004–2017   45,000–79,000
- Boko Haram, Nigeria   2009–present   52,000
- Wars in Libya   2011–present   25,000 +
- Syrian Civil War   2011–present   570,000
- Iraqi Civil War   2014–2017   195,000–200,000
- Yemeni Civil War   2015–present   112,000

There were at least fifty-eight such conflicts after 1945, with forty-three of them civil and fifteen involving states.

One worrisome aspect of wars after 1945 has been the number involving the United States. Korea, Vietnam, Afghanistan, Iraq, Libya, and Syria have all been significant both in terms of casualties and duration. Associated with such wars is the willingness of the United States to make large enemies out of small countries. Cuba, Nicaragua, Iran, and Venezuela have and continue to be preoccupations of American foreign policy, and for the most part, they are not worthy of this attention. The invasions of Grenada (1983) and Panama (1989) might be included in this categorization except the resulting regime change in Panama did allow the Americans to fulfill their treaty obligation to return the Panama Canal to Panamanian sovereignty in 2000. Sometimes tolerance or indifference creates fewer casualties in the collective response to the idiosyncratic, and at times, brutal behaviour of some leaders.

During this same period, the Soviets/Russians were involved in a lesser number of conflicts, and for the most part, these have not been far from its borders. However, in the last few years there have been exceptions, with the Russian decision to assist President Bashar al-Assad in Syria in his civil war, and taking sides in the still evolving situation in Libya. The British and French have largely kept their militaries at home and foreign adventures have been few except for participation in the wars following the breakup of Yugoslavia. Both countries have provided military support to former colonies in Africa, but these have been infrequent and obtained little attention. Britain created some measure of its former glory when it was able to turn back the forces of Argentinian "aggression" with the Falklands War. This war gave Margaret Thatcher another electoral victory and ongoing support for her destruction of the British economy. Nobody cried for Argentina, and before long, its puffed-up generals disappeared.

China has been the most circumspect of countries in its use of its military power. There were short wars with India (1962), Russia (1969), and Vietnam (1979), but the most significant was its overwhelming and deciding support in 1950 for North Korea. Its intervention then gave us the Korean Peninsula of today.

In the creation of the United Nations, a fundamental aspect was the requirement of member states to provide armed forces in support of Security Council decisions relating to wars and acts of aggression. Since then, there have been some seventy UN peacekeeping missions, the first in 1948 with the deployment of military observers to the Middle East to monitor the armistice between Israel and its Arab neighbours. Other missions authorized by the Security Council have gone to 120 countries and involved hundreds of thousands of military, police, and other personnel. Over three thousand have died in these UN operations.

In the 1990s, following the collapse of the Soviet Union, the Security Council decided to create peacekeeping forces in the disintegrating Yugoslavia, the racially torn Rwanda, and in Somalia, where government had disappeared. All three missions were failures, all in their own way. Since then, the concept of UN peacekeeping has been debated, and will hopefully, in part, be recreated. If there is not peace to be maintained, as was the case in Yugoslavia, Rwanda, and Somalia, then the idea of peacekeeping needs reinterpretation. This has happened to some extent, but the era of numerous and relatively small conflicts continues to grow, which strains both the concept of peacekeeping and the resources necessary for effective countering action. Nevertheless, the concept finds validation today with over one hundred thousand UN personnel on the ground in the Western Sahara, Central African Republic, Mali, Democratic Republic of the Congo, Sudan/Darfur/Abyei, Syria/Golan, Cyprus, Lebanon, Kosovo, South Sudan, India, Pakistan, and the Middle East.

To Die or Not to Die

Apart from its role in the creation and maintenance of peace, today the United Nations finds additional controversy in its responsibility for international public health. The World Health Organization (WHO), with its 194 members, is the most representative of all UN bodies. During periods of new diseases raging across the world, some find reasons to question the WHO's ability to provide the level of leadership needed. In all UN activities, those doing the questioning quickly subsume their own responsibilities and engage in self-indulgent criticism and actions.

At the same time, the changing relationships between the great powers has become manifest. In 2002–2003, as the SARS pandemic surged, there was a willingness for the United States and China to cooperate in seeking solutions. It was thought the experience then would extend to the needed cooperation today to manage the COVID-19 pandemic. That has not happened. Instead, the United States, in an act of ultimate self-indulgent pique, decided to withdraw from the WHO effective July 2021, arguing that the WHO is kowtowing to China. Equally, China has refused to grant permission today for Taiwan to be party to COVID-19 discussions at the WHO. China gave such permission earlier from 2009 to 2016 when Taiwan's experience in pandemics was of value. In the past and on several occasions, Taiwan joined the WHO and other UN bodies as "Chinese Taipei." Unfortunately, that level of cooperation is not present today as China and the United States misuse UN bodies in the game of zero point scoring.

Of course, in such matters it is the UN that suffers, and the UN's effectiveness is questioned during times of crisis. This is not to deny the need for organizations like the WHO to periodically update their structure and leadership. There is time for that, but it is foolhardy to do so when there is a need for collective cooperation to keep a boat's internal water level low enough to ensure flotation. Countries that believe there is short-term political advantage to be gained in questioning the WHO's value should visit Melbourne, Texas, Spain, or Canadian long-term care homes during COVID-19 for an awakening.

Back to the Future

As this account demonstrates, the global agenda is neither small nor short. Equally, at a time when great power relationships are under strain and reordering, the need for a revalidation of global will, as evident in the concluding years of the Second World War, is larger than ever. This book details these great, shifting power relationships, and towards the end provides suggestions for what should be done. In anticipation, below is a précis of those pages. It includes actions that Canada, as an example, might take to resolve its current issues with China and prepare for a future in which the Middle Kingdom will loom large.

China is the world's most dynamic and significant political and economic power. In less than forty years it has risen from being a minor irritation politically, and inconsequential economically, to a country that is central to most global issues and concerns.

China's rise came with the support, encouragement, and cooperation of most of the world's nations. Today, China cooperates with Chile in Antarctica, and sails the Arctic seas in anticipation that they will become future "Silk Roads." In between these polar regions, China has large and growing economic and political relationships with countries on all continents. Today, not surprisingly, its importance—and in some cases, its domination—is the starting point for most countries as they adjust and adapt to this new reality.

China's policy changes domestically and regionally have been large, coordinated, and effective in the emergence of today's China.

China in a Changing World

In large measure, China's use of its economic power internationally has been reasonably judicious and geared to attract support from a wide variety of regional countries, including those beyond East Asia.

China is united, decisive, and coherent in its approach to the world, in sharp contrast to the policies and actions of Russia and the United States.

From 1980 onwards, China's relationship with other major powers has reversed. The disintegration of the Soviet Union and re-emergence of Russia as a diminished global power has been easily accommodated and co-opted by China. Today, their bilateral relationship is better than at any time since Mao Zedong and Nikita Khrushchev/Leonid Brezhnev cooperated on nuclear weapons and differed on Czechoslovakia.

China's relationship with the United States is undergoing a sharp reversal. President Richard Nixon's visit to Beijing in 1972 and China's willingness at that time to cooperate with the United States in great power relationships is little mentioned or remembered. Instead, in the United States there is a growing belief in the need to "repivot" American global policies, including military assets, to Asia in order to constrain China.

As well, today the global economic powerhouse represented by China is unacceptable to the United States and there are efforts to see it diminished.

In July 2020, American Secretary of State Mike Pompeo stated after a meeting with UK Prime Minster Boris Johnson: "We want every nation to push back against the Chinese Communist Party in every dimension [. . .] I hope we can build a coalition." This is a rhetorical lament lacking in reality and substance. If ever there was a case of trying to return the wandering cow to the barn, this is the most hopeless, if not plaintive, call to action the world has seen for some time.

As for the rest of the world, which has benefited significantly from the emergence of China onto the world stage, some countries look nervously at their economic dependency. Most others will see little reason to change or adjust their growing, beneficial economic relationship with China.

The most fundamental issue remains. China's long-term strategic objective is to eliminate the activities of the United States Armed Forces from its contiguous seas and curtail its role as the security guarantor for several countries of the region, especially Taiwan. In a perverse way, over recent years, the United States' policies in the Asia-Pacific region have given indirect and direct encouragement, if not support, to the objectives of China, and have undermined its own reliability as a guarantor of security for countries in the region.

For Canada, there is an urgent need for the government to revisit its ineffective and potentially self-injurious policy with respect to the American request for the extradition of Huawei chief financial officer Meng Wanzhou and the return of two Canadians, Michael Kovrig and Michael Spavor, who are imprisoned in China. The use of the "rule of law" and the "non-payment of ransoms," central to the government's policy, is of little to no value in dealing with Beijing.

As a backup, many Canadians have urged the government to euphoniously "get tough" with China in the hope this will deliver the desired result of seeing Kovrig and Spavor returned to Canada. What the "tough" would consist of has been absent from these urgings, as there is nothing in the relationship that could be seen in Beijing as being "tough." All this might fulfill is the need of some Canadians to be seen as "doing something," but it is self-injurious and will do nothing for Kovrig and Spavor.

The essence of a policy that offers a large measure of success has been recommended by other Canadians and involves the exchange of prisoners. More generally, it reflects the actions of other countries when facing situations similar to the problem Canada has with China.

This approach requires the government to explore with Beijing the possibility of a prisoner exchange in which Meng would be allowed to return directly to China, and Kovrig and Spavor would be released and allowed to return directly to Canada. The application of the rule of law in the release of Meng would conform to the existing legal provisions of the Canadian Extradition Act. It is hoped these discussions are already underway with China.

Such exchanges with many variations have been used by governments throughout the ages and there would appear to be little reason why Beijing would not welcome such an approach. The possibility of retaliation by the United States is minimal at this time with the preoccupation offered by the November 3, 2020 elections and the United States' use of such exchanges on numerous other occasions.

There is a global need for a new approach to deal with and adjust to ascendant new powers. The old approach saw the use of empire, hegemony, domination, and containment. China represents a situation where power is centred on economic and political cooperation, and not military. In the absence of an identifying concept, this might be called *Realistic Engagement.*

There are two large events that make the development of policy on the new China particularly hazardous. The immediate one is the continuing effects of the global coronavirus pandemic. It is relatively early days in the life of the still rampaging virus, its treatment, and the development of effective vaccines.

There are early signs that many countries are successfully dealing with the virus, but it will be many months before these signs are conclusive. There are also signs that some countries, notably the United States, Brazil, Russia, and India, are encountering major difficulties in controlling the spread of the virus. While these difficulties are largely internal to the policies of the countries themselves, their overall significance to the global effort will continue to cause considerable pause in seeing the virus effectively dealt with on a global basis.

The second major event in the development of policy towards the new China, which in many ways is a reflection of ancient China, is the November 3, 2020 presidential and congressional elections in the United States. Today, the elements of President Donald Trump's re-election campaign relate to the success of the American economy despite the effects of COVID-19, the need for law and order in dealing with the numerous political and social divides in the country, and the negative role of China on both COVID-19 and the economic problems the United States will continue to encounter.

For the Democrats under Joe Biden, the central themes include the disastrous mismanagement by President Trump of the COVID-19 pandemic, the president's erosion of the economic well-being of millions of Americans and his support for policies that further endanger the lives of Americans, and China's future global role.

The re-election of President Trump will see the continuation and intensification of his first-term policies that undermined the collective efforts of allies to deal with many of the world's problems, including climate change, global trade rules and reductions in American forces overseas, a closer relationship with Russia under Vladimir Putin, and further confusion in relations with China and countries in the Asia-Pacific region.

The election of a President Biden would see efforts to return the United States to its historical constructive and helpful role in the management of the world. This would include the return of the United States to playing a central role on climate change, trade rules, and supporting the United Nations more generally. As well, there would be little effort to construct a better relationship with Russia, and instead, support for Eastern European countries would intensify.

It is uncertain what position Biden would take on China. There are indications he is assuming an ascendant China would be inimical to the policies he would promote. However, one aspect of the presidency under Biden would be the return of a more coherent foreign policy for the United States in line with the belief that American exceptionalism must be maintained. However, an antagonistic approach to China would be of little value in a world where most countries would not be supportive.

It can be assumed that former president Barack Obama would play a significant role in a Biden administration.

In this age of rising, falling, and confusing roles of the countries that have dominated the international concourse for the past seventy or so years, there is a need for others to come forward and provide coherence and construction in global management. There are many countries, including Canada, that could provide leadership, initiative, and resources in such an effort.

The European Union, with its successful containment of the gap left by the departing United Kingdom, the use of its enormous economic power to assist all in the recovery from the coronavirus pandemic, and the early return to its borderless internal freedom of travel and historical connections to all corners of the world, offers the opportunity for global leadership. It would be a leadership grouping countries such as Canada, Japan, Brazil, Nigeria, South Africa, Egypt, India, Algeria, Jamaica, Norway, Indonesia, and Turkey.

The first step for such a coalition—tentatively called *United Democracies*—would be to establish the basic understanding that the historical concepts of empire, hegemony, domination, and containment would not be elements in new global cooperative initiatives. The second step would be to re-establish the sanctity of national boundaries and seek the reversal of recent changes achieved through aggression, either direct or indirect. The only acceptable changes to national boundaries would be those sanctioned by consultation and freely given consent.

Associated with the formation of such a coalition would be a commitment to give form and substance to international efforts supporting the emergence of the world's Indigenous peoples as full participants in all global cooperation initiatives. The United Nations Declaration on the Rights of Indigenous Peoples (UNDRIP) should be enshrined and reflected in the large unifying documents establishing the standards of national and international conduct.

Other needed initiatives would include:
- Review and establishment of new rules for war and global violence;
- Revitalization of climate change efforts and the United States' return to these discussions;
- Reactivation of the World Trade Organization (WTO) in all global trade matters;
- Examination of the role of nuclear weapons and the re-energization of efforts to reduce their numbers and the number of states holding them;
- Re-entry of the United States into the Trans-Pacific Partnership and efforts to have China become a signatory;
- Examination of the role of the UN Security Council;
- Examination of the World Health Organization's role before, during, and after pandemics and its relationship with member states;

- Expansion of existing treaties dealing with the waters of the world to include the high seas and controls on indiscriminate fishing;
- Improved international rules for internal and international political refugees;
- Improvements in the international agreements on consular matters; and
- International governance for the technical systems supporting international communications and agreements on limiting and eliminating "fake news" content initiated by governments.

2. The Global Stage – the Power of Power

> *The United States' well-established and cultivated ability to lead the world has faded into ignobility*

There are fundamental changes underway in the world's great power relationships. The post-war arrangements structured around the bipolar United States–Soviet Union relationship have largely disappeared. The Soviet Union and its seventy-year experiment in statism crumbled following its ten-year military disaster in Afghanistan, questionable economic progress, public unrest and protests from its forced "allies" in eastern Europe, and its gerontocracy in ideas and leaders. Russia now has the relevance it had before the 1917 Revolution when the men of cold power took over from the murdering and, in turn, murdered the Romanov family. Russia is a European-centered state, not unlike the United Kingdom, Germany, and France. Its sizeable military forces, nuclear arsenal, and makeshift, opportunistic alliance with China ensures Russia a place in most discussions on global matters.

In the aftermath of the disintegration of the Soviet empire in Europe and Central Asia in 1989–1991, the United States was briefly not only the preeminent global power, but the only global power. As with all giants, both in mythology and reality, the United States abandoned many of its normal cautions in dealing with others and became the world's power-drunk bully. The invasion of Afghanistan, the war on terrorism, the establishment of a place of official torture at Guantanamo Bay, the creation of an imaginary enemy in Saddam Hussein and the invasion of Iraq, the ambiguity in dealing with "Arab Spring" uprisings in Syria and Egypt, and the air-based war for regime change in Libya with the death of Muammar Gaddafi combined to overload American global management circuits and the people themselves. The United States' well-established and cultivated ability to lead the world faded into ignobility.

The American foreign policy disasters were accompanied and accentuated by domestic policies enlarging the economic, societal, and psychological chasms and abysses of American society. The election of successive congresses with agendas heavily influenced by the interests of a plebeian business class and the erosion of social safeguards led to a one-percent society of and for the rich. Many of the long-standing consensuses of American society became unbridgeable.

The list of internal American divisive debates is a long one: the fantasy-driven banking disaster of 2008; the debilitating debates around Supreme Court membership and its disappearance as a place of reason; the muddling into immigration and creating walls without reason; the erosion of the sound historical constitutional divide between church and state with emphasis on "social" issues involving personal choice, taste, and consciousness; the cultivation of the gun fetish; the use of the "war" metaphor as an escape for all societal problems; the elimination of "proud" from the vocabulary of Indigenous peoples; and, above all, the inability of the two "founding" peoples—European and African—to live side by side with their differences of race and colour. All of these debates contribute to a constant and debilitating daily grind within the American political system.

The 2008 election of the first Black president, Barack Obama, a monumental event of broad national and international importance, was, in and of itself, not a welcomed leap into the future. Rather, it deepened long-standing chasms in American society. While the eight years of the Obama administration were, in the main, a reflection of the sensible middle of American politics, Obama's successor in the White House reflected the worst of American politics. It hastened the erosion of American influence throughout the world.

In 1958, at the peak of American power and with the Vietnam War not yet an American national disaster, the novel *The Ugly American* by Eugene Burdick was published. There was worldwide reaction and "the ugly American" became a trope both for Americans and the world. It illustrated the dark side of American power, and politically, it led to a limited and partial self-examination by America of its role in the world. With the election of Donald J. Trump in 2016, we now understand how limited that examination was as the ugliest aspects of the American persona were set loose on the world. Trump, a man of little knowledge who is crude, rude, and mean, waves an imaginary policy wand, expecting that something magical will happen. The world shudders.

When one superpower, the Soviet Union, has disappeared, leading to independence, democratic governance, and significant economic improvements for many countries, and the ongoing self-destruction of another, the United States, it sets the stage for the new centre of global power and influence to enter. That new centre is China. Significantly different in many ways from its two predecessors, China is today confidently acting as a major power on the global stage. It certainly has the attributes that fully support its superpower status: non-Western, ancient in its existence, a large well-educated population, social coherence and unity, economically practical and dominant worldwide, a military modernized with nuclear weapons, and an ability to wander the heavens with its own brands of rocketry.

However, it is not a superpower without serious faults and limitations. Its non-democratic, highly sequestered and secretive governmental structures supported by large dedicated security and military organizations have served a small, self-selecting leadership well in the years since the 1949 Chinese Communist Revolution. China's status has been enhanced through the most temporal of human inventions: money.

It is a familiar system in Chinese history. The centrality of all authority "under heaven" (or in Chinese, *Tianxia*) provided the country with widespread progress and relative peace over thousands of years while the rest of the world was coping with or emerging from dark or semi-dark eras. A substantial inventory of the Chinese origins of many of the concepts and inventions associated with European and Arab progress was made by Joseph Needham in his monumental work *Science and Civilisation in China*. It provides a detailed understanding of the Chinese origins of these concepts and inventions and has yet to be challenged in any effective way.

The rise and fall of empires and civilizations is a familiar subject in Western literature and gives reason to believe there is no absolute immobility in the Chinese system. Associated with present-day China is the transformation of a society historically centred on villages and farms. Today, as with most modern societies, China is an urban society of well-educated persons, with many striving for individual security and expression. The urban majority emerged less than a decade ago.

The millions of Chinese educated both in China and abroad, the extensive travel by millions more, and the migration of fifty million more Chinese around the globe are significant characteristics of modern China. There are ten or so countries with a million or more persons of Chinese descent, and twenty or more with significant such populations. There are also twenty-three million Chinese in Taiwan, six to seven million more in each of Hong Kong and Singapore, and about two hundred thousand in Macau. The number of Chinese students at Western schools (pre-COVID-19) is in the millions. In Canada alone, they are estimated at close to two hundred thousand. Chinese students are an important factor, both intellectually and financially, in the well-being of these institutions. The growth of internal transportation and the spread of communications, both domestically and internationally, have also unified China, and contributed to the transformation of Chinese society.

The Communist Party of China has been in existence for nearly a century. Its victory over the nationalist forces of Chiang Kai-shek in 1949 began a tumultuous period of change. The Party has survived large policy failures such as The Great Leap Forward and the Cultural Revolution; the Tiananmen Square massacre only thirty-one years ago in 1989; and, from time to time, warring leadership factions and minor wars that would have sundered lesser organizations. The one hundred million members of the Party remain as the epitome of orthodoxy, the backbone for all change and its enforcers. It remains a highly rigid system where initiative and adventure are neither rewarded nor encouraged, as the reaction to the COVID-19 outbreak in Wuhan recently demonstrated.

Political immutability during periods of large social and economic change provides little assurance of success. China's own history has more examples of this than most. While we are fixated on the scale and the speed with which China has come to dominate our world, there is no need to panic or to overreact to its effects and manifestations. A guiding principle of Western policies and actions in the coming months and years is the avoidance of doing more injury to ourselves than creating the expectation that we can influence the large changes wrought by China. Those changes, in and of themselves, will moderate China more than anything we do.

3. Beginnings – Comings and Goings of Empires

> *"All countries end. Every society has its own rock bottom, obscured by darkness until impact is imminent."* —Charles King 2020

George Kennan and Containment

In 1947, a junior official in the American embassy in Moscow, George Kennan, wrote an eight-thousand-word message to Washington. In what became known as "The Long Telegram" (or its proper name, "The Sources of Soviet Conduct"), the report provided a perceptive analysis of Soviet postwar policies, and most uniquely, the outline of policies that might be used to counter Soviet global ambitions.

Fortunately, the telegram went into a policy environment in Washington open to ideas for how to manage American postwar global hegemony. Central to Kennan's analysis was the concept of containment, not war, as the most effective response to Soviet ambitions in Europe and globally. Fortunately, the Americans had President Harry Truman and associated advisers, who were experienced in the vicissitudes of war and sensitive to ideas that would support America's own global ambitions. The subsequent creation of the European-centered Marshall Plan, the North Atlantic Treaty Organization (NATO), and the permanent stationing of American troops in western Europe provided the foundations for postwar Europe. Canadian and British troops remained stationed in western Europe for some twenty-five years after the war, contributing to its long-term peace, security, and economic progress.

China in a Changing World

The immediacy of these events offers little occasion for deep reflection or comprehensive understanding. An expression from the island of Newfoundland reflects the issue: "We are building the boat by while we sail her." The span of human life, individually, is not long and does not provide for comprehension or understanding of the large changes in our world. It is left to the historian in the afterlife of large change to provide the explanatory footnotes of what happened.

Zhou Enlai, the premier of China at the time, in a conversation with the American national security adviser Henry Kissinger, replied to a question about the effect of the French Revolution saying it was "Too early to say." Whether the story is true is still being debated, but it is an apocryphal story illustrating the problem all historians encounter when providing firm conclusions after large events. Either way, it does provide a cautionary note to those attempting some measure of understanding of the policies and actions of the government of China today. That boat is still a-building as China confidently sails it around the world.

Edward Gibbon and the Romans

Edward Gibbon did not face this problem when his magisterial books *The History of the Decline and Fall of the Roman Empire* were published in the last quarter of the eighteenth century. As with the French Revolution, the Roman Empire more than a thousand years earlier could be detailed in the cool light of considerable retrospect. But as with all history, these effects will be eternally debated to meet our own understandings and experiences, and an army of always out-of-step historians is available to ensure that we do not lack for new grist for measurement in the large wheels of the global change grind.

For Kennan, at the time he wrote his message, Adolf Hitler and Franklin Roosevelt were dead; Winston Churchill, out of office, was writing his way back to affluence and building brick walls at Chartwell; Charles de Gaulle, retired at Colombey-les-Deux-Églises having nursed his war "wounds" at the hands of *les anglais,* was plotting the death of the Fourth Republic and the birth of the fifth; and Truman, upon the death of Roosevelt in 1945, had reportedly said to the press at his swearing-in, "Boys, if you ever pray, pray for me now." Truman felt that the moon, the stars, and all the planets had fallen on him. But in Moscow, Joseph Stalin was the rock around which all Soviet power resolved, and for Western countries, he represented a large threatening force.

Unique in Kennan's telegram was the connection between analysis and policy. His work did provide a broad understanding of the new world. It also provided the foundation for the specific policies the United States and its allies could use in dealing with the Soviet Union. As Kennan wrote, the ideological, political, and economic policies of the Soviet Union needed countering as the country translated the power associated with its political success at home and its European military success into "the pursuit of unlimited authority domestically, accompanied by the cultivation of the semi-myth of implacable foreign hostility." This created the conclusion that the "aims of the capitalist world are antagonistic to the Soviet regime, and therefore to the interests of the peoples it controls." Kennan concluded that antagonism remained, and the conduct of foreign policy by the Soviet Union, "the secretiveness, the lack of frankness, the duplicity, the wary suspiciousness and the basic unfriendliness of purpose," were there to stay for the "foreseeable future."

Kennan summarized the "outstanding features of Communist thought" as

> (a) The central factor in the life of man, the factor which determines the character of public life and the "physiognomy of society", is the system by which material goods are produced and exchanged; (b) the capitalist system of production is the nefarious one which inevitably leads to the exploitation of the working class by the capital-owning class and is incapable of developing adequately the economic resources of society or of distributing fairly the material good produced by human labour; (c) capitalism contains the seed of its own destruction and must, in view of the inability of the capital-owning class to adjust itself to economic change, result eventually and inescapably in a revolutionary

transfer of power to the working class; and (d) imperialism, the final phase of capitalism, leads directly to war and revolution.

Shortly after this summarization, Kennan quotes Gibbon. Gibbon wrote in *Decline and Fall*: "From enthusiasm to imposture the step is perilous and slippery; the demon of Socrates affords a memorable instance of how a wise man may deceive himself, how a good man may deceive others, how the conscience may slumber in a mixed and middle state between self-illusion and voluntary fraud." In doing so, Kennan illustrated the fragility of ideology when political leaders translated it into political policy and action. Perhaps it is not an exaggeration to suggest that Kennan is forecasting the events of 1989 in the Soviet Union at a time when the afterglow of the extraordinary Soviet military victory in Europe was still strong. As such, it provides confidence for the measurement of large change, if not understanding, of our present phantasmagoric world.

Towards the end of his essay, Kennan writes, "but the possibility remains (and in the opinion of this writer it is a strong one) that Soviet power, like the capitalist world of its conception, bears within it the seeds of its own decay, and that the sprouting of these seeds is well advanced." It is from that firm conclusion that Kennan recommends that "the United States entering with reasonable confidence upon a policy of firm containment, designed to confront the Russians with unalterable counter-force at every point where they show signs of encroaching upon the interests of a peaceful and stable world."

In words that have relevance for not only the United States today but to our collective understanding of our future world, Kennan warns that "the issue of Soviet-American relations is in essence a test of the overall worth of the United States as a nation among nations. To avoid destruction the United States need only measure up to its own best traditions and prove itself worth of preservation as a great nation." Clearly, in 1946, American exceptionalism was the international norm, even for someone as perceptive as George Kennan. He ends his essay with the words that still echo among Americans: Americans "will rather experience a certain gratitude to a Providence which, by providing the American people with this implacable challenge, has made their entire security as a nation dependent on their pulling themselves together and accepting the responsibilities of moral and political leadership that history plainly intended them to bear."

Before leaving Gibbon and Kennan, it is worth noting another phrase from *Decline and Fall* that Kennan quotes with approval. The phrase "chastise the contumacy," in Kennan's view, reflects the in-built contradictions of all ideologically based political movements. He goes on to write that "it is an undeniable privilege of every man to prove himself right in the thesis that the world is his enemy, for if he reiterates it frequently enough and makes it the background of his conduct, he is bound eventually to be right." Fortunately, contumacy is still abundantly available.

Andrei Amalrik and the Soviets

Post-Kennan, over the next fifty years, there was considerable contumacy within the Soviet Union. Aleksandr Solzhenitsyn and Andrei Sakharov were well-known critics of the Soviet system and, along with hundreds of others, were persecuted and prosecuted by Leonid Brezhnev. They became well-known in the West, were recognized with Nobel prizes, and eventually left the Soviet Union. Another dissident, less well-known, was Andrei Amalrik, a writer who, in the late 1970s, cast his imaginative mind forward and sought to describe the future for the Soviet system. He was less sanguine than others and did not see détente, cooperation, and convergence as moderating the deep differences between the Western system of democratic capitalism and the Soviet communism. In an article smuggled out to London in late 1970, Amalrik in his title wrote "Will the Soviet Union Survive Until 1984?"

Charles King, a professor at Georgetown University, in an article for *Foreign Affairs* published June 30, 2020 titled "How a Great Power Falls Apart," closely examines the prescience of Amalrik's writing in 1970 with an eye on the need for similar prescience today. King writes:

China in a Changing World

Viewed from 2020, exactly 50 years since it was published, Amalrik's work has an eerie timeliness. He was concerned with how a great power handles multiple internal crisis – the faltering of institutions of domestic order, the craftiness of unmoored and venal politicians, the first tremors of systemic illegitimacy. He wanted to understand the dark logic of social dissolution and how discrete political choices sum up to apocalyptic outcomes. His prophecy was time delimited, ending in 1984 but it isn't hard to hear its ghostly echo today. To know how great powers end, one could do worse than study the last one that actually did.

In interpreting Amalrik, Professor King sees closer proximity to the views of Gibbon than those of Kennan in understanding why great powers fall. King writes, "it was a great mistake, Amalrik continued, to believe that one could make political predictions about a country surveying its main ideological currents. People might cleave themselves into rival camps [. . .] but these groups are always amorphous. Their constituents display little real agreement among themselves about what constitutes orthodox belief or a coherent political program."

With an eye firmly on Washington today, Professor King concludes his essay:

> All countries end. Every society has its own rock bottom, obscured by darkness until impact is imminent. As a theorist of his own condition, he [Amalrik] was in many ways a fatalist. He believed that the Soviet Union lacked the nimbleness to engage in system-shaking reform and still survive, and he was correct. But his broader contribution was to show the citizens of other, differently structure countries how to worry well. He offered a technique for suspending one's deepest political mythologies and posing questions that might seem, here and now, to lie at the frontier of crankery.

One last note on historical treatises. Ideology is an important aspect in Kennan's description of Soviet policy as it provides the cement for the dual concepts of domestic control and worldwide revolution to co-exist. However, ideology plays no role in Gibbon's *Decline and Fall*. For Gibbon, "history is, indeed, little more than the register of the crimes, follies and misfortunes of mankind," forming the cement upon which his comprehensive writings on why the empire called Rome fell. At the time Gibbon wrote, the word *ideology* did not exist as it was only during and after the French Revolution of 1789 that it obtained currency. Volumes IV, V, and VI of *Decline and Fall* were published in 1788–1789. Today, unfortunately, ideology has become a word of immense scope, confusion, and misuse. Except in a few cases, it has become a go-to word to describe the follies of individuals, their would-be saviours, and their societies. It continues to distort more than it illuminates.

In reflecting on these historical assessments of the fall and demise of large, dominating countries, and as is demonstrated later with respect to the United States, their disasters are largely the result of internal problems. While the decline of Rome was hastened with the arrival of North African elephants on their doorsteps, the problems encouraging the Carthaginians to show up had very much to do with the internal corruption of Rome itself. Similarly, with the Soviet Union it was the bankruptcy of both its ideology and leadership that created conditions that could no longer be controlled. Equally, with the United States, the long series of lost wars, fought largely over American angsts; the transfer of wealth to a few; and an unwillingness to provide justice to all combined to produce a leadership totally out of tune with the country and a changed world. It would not be a large projection to suggest that China, in time, will succumb to some of these same pressures that have sundered other countries recently and at times long ago.

4. Back to China and When Today Started

> *In today's world, the exceptionalism espoused by the United States is a distortion. For China, exceptionalism is a coat worn with historical confidence.*

In understanding the China of today, there is one sharp difference from what George Kennan was describing in the Soviet Union, and it relates to ideology. Marxism-Leninism, while foreign to China, still played a role in providing cohesion for the Communist Party of China in the days before its ultimate success in 1949. As in the Soviet Union, it provided the cement holding together the disparate forces of revolution that promised a better future. But with victory, it soon had a new face—one of a living leader rather than ones long dead, as in the Soviet Union. The indigenization of Marxism-Leninism through Maoism provided the basis for both change and political opposition, ultimately leading to the emergence of a China today where ideology has little to do with its policies and actions. Edward Gibbon would be completely at home in writing about China using his perspective that "history is, indeed, little more than the register of the crimes, follies and misfortunes of mankind."

Fast-forwarding to today, the experience from that postwar period remains of some relevance to the current inchoate approach by the world to the emergence of China as a superpower. Nowhere is that more evident than with the Western democracies. The difference is that the Soviet Union never represented an economic threat in the postwar growth of Western and global economies. While China is not a military threat as such, it is an enormous factor in the world's economy. Unfortunately, the successful 1949 communist revolution in the world's most populous country began an era of confusion, in the United States and elsewhere, on policies to deal with the world's longest-existing coherent country. The silliness of that confusion was best reflected in the United States, where hundreds of officials and others were accused of and punished for "losing China."

The Western defeat on the Korean peninsula and Alvin Hamilton's actions on behalf of Canada's John Diefenbaker government in 1960 to begin wheat sales to China illustrates the ambiguity in such policies. Ten years later, Canada "officially" recognized Beijing and re-established an embassy in China. The confusion and ambiguity for many came to an end two years later, in 1972,when President Richard Nixon provided American legitimacy by visiting Beijing.

Today, China is the world's largest trading country and its economic policies over the past four decades have seen hundreds of millions emerge from poverty and become some of the world's most ubiquitous tourists and students, and at home, efficient workers. Importantly, in this process, for many countries, including the United States, China became a significant factor in their own economic well-being. Accompanying its successful post-Mao economic revolution, unsurprisingly, China has promoted and exploited its national, regional, and global status. Key to these policies is the restoration of its long-lived belief of the centrality of China to the history of the world.

The battering of this belief by European colonial powers in the eighteenth and nineteenth centuries, and the invasion by Japan in the twentieth, are wounds that are yet to completely heal. It adds to the heft of China's attitude towards much of the world. The idea that China is a country like all others is not one that is argued in Beijing and offers no help for understanding its policies and actions. It was not an abstraction that China self-identified as "the Middle Kingdom." In today's world, the exceptionalism espoused by the United States is a distortion. For China, exceptionalism is a coat worn with historical confidence.

5. Lots of Borders – Some Compromises but No Need to Fight

> *For Tokyo, Seoul, Moscow, New Delhi, Canberra, Washington, or Ottawa, the policies of the new China cannot be understood singularly from what has happened recently; rather, they are the renewal of policies originating in the long history of China.*

The ebb and flow of territory has been a neuralgic factor in the dynastic history of China. It remains today one of the hardest of rocks in the policies of Beijing. China has land boundaries with fourteen countries, second only to Russia in such a measure, and marine "boundaries" with ten more. Not surprisingly, Taiwan, in its Republic of China guise, claims marine boundaries similar to those of the mainland and there are few differences in its views on land boundaries.

Contentions with or over Taiwan, Tibet, Hong Kong, Xinjiang (and the Chu Valley), India and Aksai Chin, Bhutan, Mongolia, Vietnam, Russia, Siberia, and North Korea are all issues that, in one way or another, are not open for negotiations but are absolutes as Beijing faces the world. Even the certainty of a settlement does not carry ease of mind in neighbouring capitals as uncertainty, or in the view of some, inscrutability, remains an important element in Chinese policy. It should be emphasized that "inscrutability" is not pejorative; rather, it is the ability to use the fullness available with time to your own advantage. For Tokyo, Seoul, Moscow, New Delhi,

Canberra, Washington, or Ottawa, the policies of the new China cannot be understood singularly from what has happened recently; rather, they are the renewal of policies that have long existed in China.

In a recent report, the Congressional Research Service (CRS) in Washington detailed the status of the Chinese military in the aftermath of its poor performance in the war with Vietnam. Decisions in the 1990s resulted in extensive reforms and the expansion of capabilities. Its budget is estimated to be about a quarter of that of the United States', but in one significant area, its navy, its capability is larger. China's navy is now estimated to have 338 warships while the United States only has 285.

In its May 2020 report to Congress, the CRS wrote:

> In an era of renewed great power competition, China's military modernization effort, including its naval modernization effort, has become the top focus of U.S. defence planning and budgeting. China's navy, which China has been steadily modernizing for more than 25 years, since the early to mid-1990s, has become a formidable military force within China's near-seas region, and it is conducting a growing number of operations in more-distant waters, including the broader waters of the Western Pacific, the Indian Ocean, and waters around Europe. China's navy is viewed as posing a major challenge to the U.S. Navy's ability to achieve and maintain wartime control of blue-water ocean areas in the Western Pacific—the first such challenge the U.S. Navy has faced since the end of the Cold War—and forms a key element of a Chinese challenge to the long-standing status of the United States as the leading military power in the Western Pacific.

The report went on to say:

> China's military modernization effort, including its naval modernization effort, is assessed as being aimed at developing capabilities for addressing the situation with Taiwan militarily, if need be; for achieving a greater degree

of control or domination over China's near-seas region, particularly the South China Sea; for enforcing China's view that it has the right to regulate foreign military activities in its 200-mile maritime exclusive economic zone (EEZ); for defending China's commercial sea lines of communication (SLOCs), particularly those linking China to the Persian Gulf; for displacing U.S. influence in the Western Pacific; and for asserting China's status as the leading regional power and a major world power.

There are nine nuclear weapons states. Five of these—China, North Korea, Russia, Pakistan, and India—have common land borders. A sixth—the United States—has defence obligations in the region that could involve the possible use of nuclear weapons. Only three of them—China, Russia, and the United States—are signatories to the Treaty on the Non-Proliferation of Nuclear Weapons; the other three—North Korea, Pakistan, and India—are non-signatories. North Korea, having being a signatory, withdrew from the treaty in January 2003. It exploded its first nuclear device on October 9, 2006.

A review of the "neighbouring" countries near and far provides some measure of the complexity and the success the new China has had as it emerged as the major, dynamic force in today's world.

North Korea

North Korea represents the most difficult foreign policy issue for China and for the world. At times belligerent and hostile, always well-prepared militarily and adding nuclear weapons with long-range delivery systems, sometimes peacefully inclined, economically desperate with famines on every horizon, and at times having immature leaders with few friends, North Korea is one of Asia's ongoing troublesome issues. For China, North Korea's importance has not changed appreciably from 1950 when it sent a million troops into the country to counter American and UN military advances to its border. Recently, for a brief period, there was some expectation that China was willing to cooperate with Western efforts to bring some measure of control and forbearance to North Korea, especially on nuclear weapons. That did not last much beyond the cold realization in Beijing that Pyongyang was a firmly connected suburb, and while at times a troublesome close relative, it was a necessity in China's larger, longer-term objectives in the region.

North Korea has China's only mutual defence treaty, and with the American mutual defence arrangements with South Korea, it provides a four-country iron ring that will not change in the foreseeable future. While the Americans under Trump have played silly games on the issues involved, especially North Korea's nuclear program, despite the fanciful ideas of large-scale change on the Korean peninsula festering in the minds of some, nothing has changed. Rather, the China–North Korea axis has hardened. For North Korea, the reiteration of the fundamental nature of the relationship has provided opportunities for eliminating inclinations for improved relations with the South. It also permits the continuation of its nuclear weapons program and associated missile delivery system.

For South Korea, any expectations of better relations with the North are put back in the drawer where long-term dreams are stored. The importance of the American military guarantee and its associated nuclear umbrella returns as the essential element in the existence of South Korea. Unfortunately, the major uncertainty is the quality of the American guarantees, which in recent years have been subject to idiosyncratic and soft illusions about the American role in Asia. In all of this, the China–North Korea relationship will remain the hard rock around which the policies of others must navigate.

Russia

Russia, with the largest empty space in the world bordering the world's most populous country, continuously ponders Chinese northern policy. Mao's wondering out loud about Siberia still lingers and the border disputes from a few decades ago illustrate the large military problems that Russia's empty east represents for Moscow. This is not northern Georgia or Crimea or Chechnya. There is a certain element of common cause in the relationship today, especially in terms of the supply of Siberian energy into the Chinese heartland and the opening up of the Northeast Passage for Chinese shipping into Europe. There is also limited but increasing cooperation on military matters.

China in a Changing World

Driving the cooperative relationship between Russia and China today is the fractured relationship each has with the United States. Both Russia and China consider that "being friendly" on the basis of a common enemy is of value, and until there is some measure of change in the relationships with the United States, they will continue to see a quiet border and cross-border cooperation of significant value. Equally, with the prospects of presidents Xi Jinping and Vladimir Putin being around for at least another decade, the comfort they give each other will not be squandered on any long-term aspirations of geographic changes. Russia has a common border with North Korea, but there are few prospects it will make common cause with other countries in countering any actions of Pyongyang. The status quo meets Russian needs in the region, just as they meet those of Beijing.

Mongolia

Historically, Mongolia has had both highs and lows. It was the world's largest empire less than a thousand years ago, stretching from Asia into Poland and just east of Vienna, and it ruled all of China. Today it is land-locked, with three million people. Its only borders are with Russia and China, and it is dependent on both for its political and economic survival. Not much more than a hundred years ago, China considered Outer Mongolia, as it was then called, as a part of China, to be handled similar to Inner Mongolia. The latter is now the Inner Mongolia Autonomous Region, and there are fewer and fewer Mongolians. Initially, Taiwan, then acting as the Republic of China, vetoed membership for Mongolia in the United Nations, but eventually it became a member and is today part of the land-locked international caucus.

A reasonably democratic system provides representative government, and Mongolia's relationship with both Russia and China is, in comparative terms, benign. Mongolia is one of the least troublesome of China's bordering countries.

Kazakhstan, Kyrgyzstan, and Tajikistan

Only thirty-seven kilometres of Chinese territory separates western Mongolia from eastern Kazakhstan. This is an area where history and religion fuse, and for China, its ongoing efforts to pacify its own significant Muslim population make the region one of considerable importance. Equally, it is a region where the Silk Roads, past and present, converge, as the area provides for part of the land element of China's Belt and Road Initiative. The Chongqing–Xinjiang–Europe railway, which passes through Kazakhstan, is important for Chinese–European trade. The importance of China to all three countries is recognized and there are few problems of note. Borders with all three countries have been demarcated and fixed through negotiations (Kazakhstan,1,783 kilometres; Kyrgyzstan,1,063 kilometres; and Tajikistan, 477 kilometres). While the issue of China's treatment of its Muslim population creates some unease, this has not affected the countries' growing economic relationships with China.

Afghanistan

This country's border with China is only 76 kilometres, and was demarcated in 1963. There are nature reserves on both sides. The main route through the area is the Wakhjir Pass, which is considered a drug-smuggling area for Afghan opium into China. The area borders on Xinjiang, and while Afghanistan has asked for this route to be opened, China has resisted. There are indications the Taliban has been active on the Afghan side of the border. The possibility for future trouble in the area exists should an agreement between the Afghan government and the Taliban ever occur. The writ of Kabul does not run to the area and the possibility of the Taliban making common cause with their co-religionists in Xinjiang is not one Beijing would accept with equanimity.

Pakistan

Of its bordering countries, China has the most stable relationship with Pakistan. Pakistan recognized the People's Republic shortly after its formation, and over the years, the two countries have developed a broad range of cooperation on political, economic, and military matters. The common border has been demarcated, a connecting road constructed, trade expanded, and political ties enhanced. China is now the major supplier of military equipment to Pakistan, which includes assistance on nuclear and missile matters. The connecting road, the Karakoram Highway, gives China direct access to the Persian Gulf through the joint development of

Gwadar Port in southern Pakistan. Their sharing of India as a common enemy provides a dimension that continues to drive the relationship, and there are few signs this will change in the near future. Throughout these developments, Pakistan's historic relationship with the United States has eroded and it will largely disappear with the ending of American military involvement in Afghanistan, and the establishment of closer American–Indian relations.

India

There are few signs that China's relations with India will improve in the coming years. The identification of India by others as a counter to the expansion of China's influence throughout Asia has become a factor of consequence. The recent military skirmishing at Pangong Lake in Ladakh and Tibet is but one element in the larger strategic positioning. Compared to China, India is ill-prepared to act as a significant counter in the larger game. Its military could not effectively counter any large-scale action by China on the common border, there is little internal coherency, and its economic growth, while dynamic, has ignored over two-thirds of its people, who continue to live in conditions not much improved since Indian independence in 1947. The ruling Bharatiya Janata Party's use of Hindu nationalism, or "Hinduness," as an electoral strategy to win elections has alienated many and erodes, for the near term, the emergence of a coherent view on India's relations within the region and the world.

Nepal

Land-locked Nepal, with only two neighbouring countries, India and China, is an important cog in the competition for dominance in the Great Himalayas. Its border with China was demarcated in 1960. Nepal's historic religious ties with neighbouring Tibet have largely eroded, but the establishment of transportation connections provides an alternative to the traditional ones with India. India has used its transportation connections to pressure Nepal, but in doing so, provided Nepal with the need to improve ties with China. A railway now connects Lhasa in Tibet with the border and plans are underway for it to be extended to Kathmandu. Tens of thousands of Nepalis work and live in India and their remittances provide Nepal with an important source of funds. Equally, thousands of Indians have migrated into southeastern Nepal, providing a large irritant in the relationship with China.

Bhutan

Bhutan is the only country that does not have formal diplomatic relations with either Beijing or Taipei. Its border with China is not yet demarcated but efforts are underway to do so. In the meantime, China has built roads in the border area and will continue to do so as long as the border remains in dispute. There is a 1998 Agreement on the Maintenance of Peace and Tranquility, but so far it has not led to a defined border. In late July 2020, China made a new offer to settle border issues, involving the exchange of land. However, the exchange would improve China's military position with respect to India, and most likely would not be acceptable. Bhutan's ties with India are close and India is supportive of Bhutan's continued independence.

Bangladesh

Bangladesh does not have a common border with China. Yet, it plays an important role in regional relationships given its former status as part of Pakistan, and is now very much a part of India's sphere of influence. It only has borders with India and Myanmar, but has sought a closer relationship with China in order to moderate Indian influence and control. Chinese military cooperation has expanded in recent years and Bangladesh's armed forces have sourced considerable equipment from China. The dispute with Myanmar, with the forced exiling of tens of thousands of former Bengalis back into Bangladesh, continues. There are few signs many will ever return to their former homes in Myanmar.

Sri Lanka

A few years ago, analysts of geopolitical vision and insight thought they were witnessing a large pattern emerging with China's activities in the Indian Ocean. These activities consisted of a network of Chinese military and commercial facilities supporting its sea lanes out of the South China Sea across the Indian Ocean and into Africa and the Mediterranean via the Suez Canal. The network of ports was quaintly dubbed the "String of Pearls," but in reality, it reflected the ancient Maritime Silk Road of China. Four of the most important "pearls" include the port facilities at Kyaukpyu in Myanmar, at Hambantota in southern Sri Lanka, Gwadar in Pakistan, and Obock in Djibouti. India was quick to realize these facilities, in addition to their importance to China's exports and import of oil from the Middle East, could be of considerable military value in any potential conflict in the Indian Ocean. An examination of the development of the facilities at Hambantota in Sri Lanka illustrates the fragility of this concept without denying the value of its underlying premise.

Sri Lanka has only recently emerged from a brutal, almost thirty-year civil war, and the tsunami of December 2004 further ravaged the country. The small island, only 1,700 kilometres from the epicentre of the massive underwater earthquake in western Sumatra, was inundated two hours afterwards by nine-metre waves along its eastern coast and, subsequently, around its southern reaches. Hambantota was devastated, with over 4,500 people killed.

In the aftermath, Colombo initiated efforts to redevelop the area, including a new international port consisting of a tax-free zone, shipbuilding and repair facilities, bunkering, and warehousing. It is now largely complete. Chinese companies were involved in the development and construction of the port and other facilities, and in 2017 the government entered into a ninety-nine-year lease with China's Merchant Port Holdings in order to reduce the associated onerous debt. In doing so, the Sri Lankan government achieved considerable relief from its debts with China, although there is a fair amount of unease with the length of the lease, and a recently elected government announced it would try and change the lease's terms. Most observers do not foresee the lease being changed.

The Hambantota situation is somewhat characteristic of similar problems in the development of Chinese port facilities in Myanmar and Malaysia. In reality, they do not differ in context with large infrastructure projects elsewhere, except that in the Indian Ocean, there is the added dimension of future Chinese intentions. In a study on "Chinese Investment and BRI in Sri Lanka," published on March 24, 2020, Chatham House concluded:

> The pattern of Chinese investment in Sri Lanka reveals a nuanced picture of benefits and costs. Similarly, it shows

that a matrix of Sri Lanka, Chinese and multilateral policies are required to maximize the benefits and minimize any risks of Chinese investment. Sri Lanka is not in a Chinese debt trap. Its debt to China amounts to about 6 percent of its GDP. However, Sri Lanka's generally high debt levels show the country needs to improve its debt management systems. This step would also reduce any risk of a Chinese debt trap in the future.

Concerns that China will use ports and other projects for military purposes are, in part, driven by geopolitical anxieties. In response, Sri Lanka has strengthened its naval presence at Hambantota port. Continual oversight by technical experts is required to guard against security-related concerns and ensure public trust in the projects.

Myanmar

> *Ship me somewheres east of Suez, where the best is like the worst,*
> *Where there aren't no Ten Commandments an' a man can raise a thirst;*
> *For the temple-bells are callin', an' it's there that I would be*
> *By the old Moulmein Pagoda, looking lazy at the sea;*
> *On the road to Mandalay,*
> *Where the old Flotilla lay,*
> *With our sick beneath the awnings when we went to Mandalay!*
> *O the road to Mandalay,*
> *Where the flyin'-fishes play,*
> *An' the dawn comes up like thunder outer China 'crost the Bay!*

Rudyard Kipling's Burma was somewhat different in 1890 when this piece of British imperial doggerel was published. Yet one aspect echoes today. While the dawn could come up "outer China 'crost the Bay" poetically, geographically it was five hundred miles north of Mandalay. But in present-day Myanmar, dawn does come from China, as it is one of the few countries that maintains an improving relationship with Myanmar. A few years ago, Myanmar's military dictatorship showed signs of emerging into some semblance of representative government, with the world's favourite democrat, Aung San Suu Kyi, playing a large role. But today, a hard military face is all there is to see.

Myanmar, strategically, is as important to China as is Pakistan, and despite what is at times a troublesome relationship, China has exhibited forbearance as it establishes transportation links into the Indian Ocean. As well, the systemic unrest in the bordering Myanmar states of Kachin and Shan—with strong ties to neighbouring Yunnan—while relatively quiescent, remains a source of friction. China is the major, if not the singular, supplier of military equipment, and Myanmar in turn supports China's hard line towards the Uyghurs. But the ultimate objectives for China are the transportation links and ports on the Bay of Bengal that stare down on the east coast of India. Despite disputed financial arrangements associated with the construction of the port facilities at Kyauk Pye in Rakhine State, these will continue. This port's purpose is for the import of oil and gas from the Middle East and onward transport by pipeline into China. Myanmar's military leaders understand the possible larger Chinese objective with this port and have sought to balance this with better ties with India.

Laos

Despite its location, Laos has been relatively slow in developing a close relationship with China. Historically, Laos favoured ties with neighbouring Thailand and Vietnam, and ideologically, with the former Soviet Union. The Vietnamese invasion of Cambodia in 1975, war with China in 1979, and their continuing differences gave Laos little manoeuvring room. This is changing and China has initiated large transportation projects as part of its Belt and Road Initiative. Railway and road connections from China are under construction and a variety of resource development projects are planned. The common border has been demarked.

Cambodia

Cambodia does not have a common border with China but has been a significant player in the region. China supported the Khmer Rouge in the Cambodian Civil War, and in part, invaded Vietnam to force its withdrawal from Cambodia. Since those tumultuous days of genocide and countrywide chaos, Cambodia has emerged as a relatively moderate country in regional activities. Hun Sen, the long-time leader and former member of Khmer Rouge, has re-established a close relationship with China and the country maintains a full range of economic and military ties. There is massive investment from China in the Cambodian economy and a significant Chinese population. China's activities have moderated Vietnamese influence in the country and has helped in its ongoing border dispute with Thailand. Cambodia has severed all links with Taiwan and supports the reunification of Taiwan and China.

Thailand

Thailand's extensive role in the Vietnam War is still of some consequence, but the withdrawal of the Americans in 1975 and the increasing economic importance of China has provided Thailand the opportunity for a moderating role in the Association of Southeast Asian Nations (ASEAN)region and elsewhere in Asia. Thailand's inability to provide a stable domestic political environment has undermined its capacity to play a larger role in the region, as its military continues to dominate domestically. The king, Vajiralongkorn, who was crowned in 2019, has demonstrated none of the leadership characteristics of his father and there is a sense of drift in the country. It does not have a border with China but there is a significant population of Chinese descent.

Vietnam

A 2018 study in the *Journal of Conflict Resolution* on Vietnam–China relations from 1365 to 1841 characterized the relationship as a "hierarchic tributary system" where the "Vietnamese court explicitly recognized its unequal status in its relations with China through a number of institutions and norms."

Times have changed since the days of a "hierarchic tributary system." In spite of the extensive assistance and support from China to North Vietnam during the war, it is a troubled relationship today. Things are as bad as or worse than with any other bordering country, even India. It is not an exaggeration to state that Vietnam's relations with the United States are better and are improving more steadily than they are with China.

The Sino-Vietnamese War in 1979, with the People's Liberation Army (PLA) invading some twenty miles into Vietnam, was the continuation of earlier periods of war with both China invading Vietnam and Vietnam invading China. During these periods there was large-scale Chinese migration that, over time, was influential in the political and economic growth of the country. European involvement with the French dominance of Indochina from the late nineteenth century dampened Chinese connections and influence. The American war, the unification of the country, and the departure of millions of Vietnamese with Chinese family connections after the war has produced a more Vietnamese Vietnam than at any point in its recent history.

The return of American influence illustrates one of the more positive aspects of American policy in the region. Today, American presence is a significant element in maintaining the existing geopolitical balance in the area, and it could, in the future, either be an element for stability or disorder. For the United States, the problems associated with closer ties were illustrated by the March 2020 visit to Da Nang by the USS *Roosevelt*, an American aircraft carrier. Despite warnings concerning the presence of the novel coronavirus (COVID-19), the American military commander in the Pacific Ocean ordered that the four-day visit should proceed. It was only the second visit by an American aircraft carrier to Vietnam since the war and it was intended as a show of military might in a region increasingly concerned with the maritime claims of China.

The coronavirus invaded the aircraft carrier, and by the time the ship had returned to Guam, the virus was extensive and little understood or appreciated in Washington. The captain's concerns, in his own view, were ignored, and he indirectly went public. The Secretary of the Navy, playing a Captain Queeg role, flew to Guam, boarded the USS *Roosevelt*, berated the crew, fired the captain, and returned to Washington, all within eighteen hours. He expected to be praised by President Trump for his forthright actions. Instead, his diatribe to the crew and their cheering of the captain as he departed the ship went public and made for a scenario that even Gilbert and Sullivan would have had difficulty replicating.

The Washington drama continued, but the captain remains fired. It was a minor event, yet the USS *Roosevelt* and the United States Navy generally lost respect from a world that expected more from an American version of today's dreadnaught. For Vietnam and for the region, this episode offers a poignant reminder of the fragility of American military effectiveness, and as they look to the future, they will plan accordingly.

The 1979 Chinese invasion of Vietnam laid waste to northern Vietnam and threatened the capital, Hanoi. Both countries deployed hundreds of thousands of troops to the region, and while there has been a common effort for economic development on both sides of the disputed border since then, it remains a place of significant tension.

In the war's aftermath, and especially with the significant improvement in Chinese-American relations, serious efforts were made by both China and Vietnam to improve relations, and in many ways, the foundations were created for a mutually beneficial bilateral relationship. However, it was not long before conflicting claims involving the Paracel and Spratly islands emerged to dominate the relationship. In recent years, Vietnam has restated its claims involving the Paracels, and it actually controls several of the Spratly islands. Oil and gas exploration by both China and Vietnam has heightened the disputes, and fishing activities have occasioned violent confrontations. Both countries have deployed large naval forces to the region and the first-built Chinese aircraft carrier has also been seen in the area.

South Korea, Japan, East Timor, Australia, and New Zealand

All five of these countries, none of which have land borders with China, are of particular importance in the emergence of China as the dominant regional power. China's support of North Korea largely guarantees North Korea's existence and survival, and its role as a continuing military threat to the South.

South Korea was the last Asian country to provide recognition to the People's Republic of China (PRC) in 1975. Since then, China and

South Korea have developed a pragmatic relationship that balances to some extent Beijing's necessary support for the North. Trade has expanded exponentially and the last serious dispute was over the decision by South Korea to deploy the Terminal High Altitude Area Défense (THAAD) system provided by the United States in 2016. THAAD is an anti-ballistic missile defence system designed to destroy short-, medium-, and intermediate-range ballistic missiles in their descent and re-entry phases. The deployment is intended to counter the nuclear threat from North Korea. China regarded the deployment as an element in its containment by the United States. Chinese displeasure manifested itself through various economic and commercial measures, and while high-level meetings between South Korean and Chinese leaders have diffused the matter, Chinese concerns remain.

The deployment of THAAD represents a significant increase in American military support for South Korea. But it has not defused increasing concern in Seoul that American support is not a "forever arrangement." That concern existed before the election of President Trump, and it has intensified and increased significantly since 2016, especially with Trump's childish efforts to make a deal with North Korea on nuclear matters. South Korea became a bit player in that short-lived melodrama. It increased the fear among many Koreans that its existence could be sacrificed on the altar of American domestic politics and not its geopolitical importance in the rise of China as a global power.

The same concern is evident in **Japan**. Japan is the main bastion for American military power in the region and the country understands historical American policy in Asia is not a guarantee for the future. Again, the problem is not one of deep analysis or understanding, but rather the vicissitudes of American politics as they emerge from the ravages of the COVID-19 pandemic and the age of Trump. As well, the projection of Chinese power throughout the world based on its economic importance is unique, and how the United States reacts is central to Japan's future policies. Japan's policy of eschewing a significant military of its own has already undergone considerable moderation and the appearance of Chinese ships and submarines in its near-waters carries with it the need for the emergence of a Japan with greater military might than the one that developed in the postwar period.

East Timor. The newest independent country in Asia, East Timor, bridges the countries of Southeast Asia and Oceania, a location that gives it an importance far beyond its size. Its independence struggle, which included an invasion and occupation by Indonesia, supported by Australia, still troubles those relationships. However, the settlement of the marine boundaries in the Timor Gap and agreement on revenue-sharing from oil and gas developments with Australia has provided some measure of calm. East Timor has observer status in both the ASEAN and the Pacific Forum. China has been involved since the Portuguese left in 1975, and has offered support and assistance on a variety of political, economic, and military matters. A small community of Chinese-Timorese is important in economic matters.

Farther away, **Australia** is still living in a fantasy world where it is hoping closer military ties with the United States will provide some measure of influence, if not protection, in the changing world of Asian power politics. For some analysts in the United States, Australia represents a better "Guam" for American forces, should that be necessary. As well, while still host to limited American forces, the Philippines is a fragile ally and not one that can be relied upon should American relations with China deteriorate further. Australia was one of the first to follow American urgings to ban the involvement of Huawei in 5G network development. There have already been missteps by Australia's leaders, generally the norm in Australian politics, which has led to a strong reaction from Beijing. The economic importance of China to Australian well-being is being laid bare daily. It illustrates the flexibility of the Chinese economy to adapt and adjust to changes in its supply lines as a punishment for policies it does not like.

Australia provides an example for many countries of Chinese economic warfare at work. There are other examples, including Canada and Sweden, but it is exemplified best in the Australian context. The extent of its success is a measure yet to be taken. The success of China's policy of pressure will only emerge within the context of the success or failure of Trump's policies against China. So far it appears American economic strength will not force change on China's pressure tactics. President Trump and, to some extent, his challenger, Joe Biden have indicated China will play a large role in the November2020 elections. In both direct and indirect ways, this will provide the measure of China's policy of bending countries like Australia to its will.

When the United Kingdom entered the European Union in 1972, the economy of **New Zealand** was shattered. Over the ensuing years, New Zealand has established strong economic relations with China, and China is today a mainstay of New Zealand's economic well-being. A free trade agreement was signed in 2008, the first for China, and it has continued to provide China with preferential access to New Zealand agricultural products. The relationship has been somewhat troubled in recent years by allegations that China was using New Zealand non-governmental organizations to support its larger political objectives in the country and the region. The same issue has emerged in other countries, including Canada, but it is not one that has found much traction. New Zealand joined Australia in 2018 in banning the use of Huawei equipment in its 5G networks.

Indonesia, the Philippines, Brunei, Malaysia, and Singapore
None of these countries have borders with China, but each are involved, in one way or another, in the unresolved marine boundary issues around the South China Sea. Historically, all have had issues involving national security with China. The 1965 coup in ***Indonesia,*** which saw former president Sukarno removed from office and the associated genocide of hundreds of thousands of Indonesians of mainly Chinese descent, resulted in the suspension of the relationship with China; relations were only re-established in the early 1980s. In the aftermath, economic and commercial relations expanded and today there is flourishing trade and economic cooperation. The marine boundary remains an important issue as it involves Chinese insistence it has historical fishing rights in the Indonesian exclusive economic zone to the north of the Natuna Islands. There have been clashes in the area in recent years and there appears to be little effort to see an early end to the issue.

Since the election of President Rodrigo Duterte in 2016, Chinese–***Philippine*** relations have improved somewhat. However, this has as much to do with the role of the United States in the Philippines and the idiosyncrasies of the president as it has to do with better relations with China. The marine boundary issues involving fishing rights near the Scarborough Shoal and oil and gas developments in the Spratly Islands remain unresolved. There have been minor clashes and despite a legal ruling on the issue by a Law of the Sea tribunal, these clashes continue to sour the overall relationship. There is a large Chinese descendent population in the Philippines.

As with the Philippines, **Brunei** has a significant Chinese descendant population. It has been relatively slow in creating economic and commercial relations with China, but in recent years these have expanded, especially in the oil and gas sector.

Twenty-five percent of **Malaysia's** population is ethnically descendants of earlier migration from China. While these people of Chinese descent formed a large part of the 1950s and 1960s insurgency, which was supported by China under Mao, since Malaysian independence this population has decreased and is less important due to migration. They still form a large part of the opposition in the Malay-dominated political system. They contribute to the political, economic, and commercial relationship with China. This relationship with China is probably the best among Southeast Asia countries, and there are few signs there will be significant disruptions in the years ahead. Even the marine boundary dispute with China is less important here than it is with other countries touching the South China Sea.

Singapore has maintained close and cooperative relations with China while at the same time offering firm support for continued American military involvement in the region. Recently, it announced an agreement with the United States for American aircraft carriers to use its port during deployments into the region. As well, it has retained close economic and commercial ties with Taiwan.

6. Beyond Asia

> *The Holy See is yet to accept the need for a change in its recognition of Taiwan.*

China's relations with countries in the Asia-Pacific region are accounted for above in considerable detail, as they form the area in which China's policies and actions have immediacy and realm. Elsewhere in this book, China's connections and activities with the United States and Canada are detailed.

Yet, China's policies and activities have importance throughout the world, which demonstrates the country's ability to exercise influence far beyond its shores. In doing so, China has created a worldwide grouping of countries that obtain benefit from Beijing and that often provide support for its policies, interests, and activities. However, there are still fourteen countries that recognize Taiwan as the government of China, nine of which are in Latin America and the Caribbean, with the remaining five in the South Pacific. Each year, another country or two shifts recognition to Beijing. The Holy See is yet to accept the need for a change in its recognition of Taiwan.

Europe

China's ties to European countries are long-standing and easily predate the wanderings of Marco Polo in the late thirteenth century. Nevertheless, Polo detailed his travels to China during the height of its Mongol Empire, and with his widely read travelogue, he created the interest that still attends things Chinese today. Interestingly, while Polo and his party travelled into China overland using what came to be known as the Silk Road, their return to Venice was by sea. They landed in Singapore, Sumatra, and Jaffna, then crossed the Arabian Sea to Hormuz Island, in present-day Iran, and then sailed home to Venice. This was a two-year voyage according to one report, and of the six hundred people who left China on fourteen ships, only eighteen survived the voyage, including Marco Polo and his two brothers.

Travel today is a little easier and the twenty-seven countries in the European Union (EU) along with others in the region represent with China the largest bloc of traders in the world. China is the EU's second-biggest trading partner behind the United States, and the EU is China's biggest trading partner. As with most countries, China has a favourable balance of trade in goods (€163.7 billion) with the EU countries, and this is only partially lessened by a favourable balance for the EU (€16.7 billion) in services. There is also a large favourable balance for China in direct foreign investments, which reached €116.3 billion in 2018.

These numbers indicate the economic exchanges are vast and highly favourable to China. As such, there are ongoing negotiations between EU countries and China with an agenda not much different than that of other countries. This includes issues such as: the lack of transparency in trade policy, industrial policies and non-tariff measures that discriminate against foreign companies; strong government intervention in the economy, giving dominant and preferential treatment to state-owned firms; and poor protection and enforcement of intellectual property rights. The EU and China have been negotiating on investments since 2013, and it was expected that there would be an agreement on investments in 2020. Regarding Huawei Technologies, EU countries have been largely agnostic and do not share the United States passion for seeing the company excluded.

The agreement in late July 2020 by EU heads of government on a stimulus package to assist its members, especially the southern tier, in their economic recovery from the coronavirus pandemic was unexpected. The agreement, a first for the EU, allows for collective borrowing on a massive scale in support of member countries. In the collectivization of the resulting debt, some suggest that it might lead to an EU-wide levy, which would again be a first for the Union. This represents a massive change in the EU's operations, and support for those who see the economic integration of Europe as the forerunner for even greater collective political integration. Coming as it does, possibly close to its successful mastering of the pandemic, it is of significance in ensuring an even more involved relationship with China.

At the political level, EU countries regularly express concern over the policies and actions of Beijing with which they disagree. However, these matters rarely go beyond expressions of concern reflecting the range of views that need to be accommodated within the EU on such matters. In an era when COVID-19 dominates the agenda for all of Europe's countries and their, as yet, aspirations for economic recovery, there will not be a willingness to become part of any coalition in significant opposition to China. The united Europe of today generally prefers the use of soft diplomacy instead of their historical hammer in resolving differences.

Across the English Channel, the same benign approach on China is not so much in evidence. Prime Minister Boris Johnson lives with the consequences of his childish endorsement and support for Brexit, and at the same time, is dealing with the COVID-19 pandemic, which seems to be a more difficult task in the United Kingdom than on the continent. The EU does not appear to be eager to see a new trade agreement with the United Kingdom, and Prime Minister Johnson's bowl of porridge is a small one—and getting smaller.

It was against this bleak landscape that the American secretary of state came calling in the last days of July 2020, looking for British support for the American diplomatic war with China and its willingness to enter into an anti-China "coalition." Prime Minister Johnson prepared for the visit by announcing that Britain would reverse its earlier position on Huawei technology for its new 5G network. But subsequently, it was reported that British officials had also told Huawei to check in with them later; thus it would appear the decision might be temporary. It is assumed that "later" refers to a time after November 3, 2020. British perfidy is still alive and well.

Latin America and the Caribbean

It is difficult to find an act of American statesmanship in the long-standing and complex set of relationships between the United

States and Latin American and Caribbean countries. One such act did occur, however, in 1979, when, in the days of a collapsing Carter administration, the United States ratified a treaty with Panama that would see the Panama Canal returned to Panamanian sovereignty in 2000. With an American invasion later arranging for the "extradition" of an American-created leader, Manuel Noriega, the treaty was implemented. Today, Panama is still a suburb of Washington, but the Canal has been expanded to ensure the efficient supply of goods from Asia are delivered to all parts of the United States and beyond.

This act of statesmanship is unusual. Latin America and the Caribbean are regions where the hard edge of American power and influence has dominated since the days of the Monroe Doctrine. Then, the young United States boldly told Europeans to stay away from the shores of the Americas. Despite the millions who have fled north, leading in many ways to a significant Hispanicization of American life, there remains in the region an inherent hope for a better tomorrow at home rather than far away. A Mexican leader some years ago sorrowfully reflected this when he commented, "So far from God and so close to the United States."

With this history, many Latin American countries welcome China's increasing interest in the region. Some also see China as a needed balance to the historic involvement of European countries, which at times has been less than helpful. Despite this, for nine countries in the region, there are still two "Chinas" in play; however, it can be expected that support for Taiwan will continue to erode as investment from and trade with China increases. China is now a permanent observer in the Organization of American States (OAS) and has joined the Inter-American Development Bank as a donor. Mexico and Chile were signatories to the Trans-Pacific Partnership Agreement, and with the withdrawal of the United States, is now part of the successor agreement. So far, only Ecuador and Uruguay have joined the Asian Infrastructure Investment Bank. Politically, China quietly supports countries having major difficulties with the United States and in small ways supports Cuba, Venezuela, and Nicaragua.

The region's trade with China has increased significantly and now is estimated to be in excess of US$150 billion. Latin American exports to China, as with many other countries, consist of raw material and commodities such as copper, iron ore, oil, and soybeans. But for Costa Rica, Mexico, and El Salvador, there have been increases in the export of manufactured goods. For Brazil, Chile, and Peru, China is their largest export market, while it is the second-largest export market for Argentina, Costa Rica, and Cuba. In turn, and as with other destinations, Chinese exports mainly consist of industrial and manufactured goods.

The negotiated end to fifty years of civil war in Colombia provided an opportunity for Colombians to engage countries beyond its dependence on the United States. China has readily responded with increases in trade and investments that are relatively significant in Latin American terms. While the United States remains first in trade with Colombia, China is now second. As well, there has been a series of Chinese investments in high-profile projects, including a metro for Bogotá, a road connecting a remote interior department with the Caribbean, and a small regional railroad. There have also been small investments in the mining and renewable energy sectors and the possibility of direct air connections have been discussed.

American involvement continues to dominate but the hard hands of the American War on Terror and the harsh, ineffective approach on drug policy have created resentment. American emphasis on the production and transportation of drugs without much effort being made at home to curtail consumption ensures that Colombian "cartels" will continue to provide grist for ongoing American involvement on a large scale. Equally, the overall security within the country remains fragile and is not helped by turmoil in neighbouring Venezuela.

In 2009, Brazil, Russia, India, and China came together to further political and economic cooperation, and in some measure to counter American and Western domination of the global economy. South Africa became the fifth member of this group in 2010, known as "BRICS" (an acronym coined to represent the names of each country involved). The collective numbers for the grouping are impressive, representing over 40 percent of the world's population and over 30 percent of the world's gross domestic product (GDP) using price parity. One of BRICS's first agreements was the creation of a multilateral New Development Bank emphasizing infrastructure projects. It was financed by $10 billion contributions from each of the five members. Brazil's inclusion in the group as the only member from the western hemisphere gave it considerable prominence. However, the group has not made a continuing collective impact on the global economy, and while it continues to meet (most recently, in a virtual setting), early excitement around its creation has cooled.

Brazil's inclusion in the group, combined with the election of a popular reformist government under Luiz Inácio Lula da Silva, led Brazilians to think they were entering a new era of progress and development. Unfortunately, the dark hand of corruption and political infighting emerged when former president Lula was imprisoned, his designated successor, Dilma Rousseff, was impeached, and the election of a populous successor, Jair Bolsonaro, created an air of bewilderment throughout the country. President Bolsonaro's impact on the country has been disastrous, with Brazil now experiencing the world's third-largest number of COVID-19 cases, a number that continues to increase and that also includes the president himself. In a scene out of Gilbert and Sullivan, the courts ordered him to wear a mask.

China and Brazil have developed extensive trade and investment relations given their respective size and complementary economies. Brazil, being the largest country in the western hemisphere after Canada and the United States, will continue to be of large interest to China, but even China is nervous about future developments involving the country given the fragility of the political system. The idea of a trans-continental "Silk Road" railway has faded into obscurity. Yet, China understands the value of time more than most nations, and in the years ahead, Brazil will re-emerge as a country of significance in China's global strategy.

In the ***Caribbean***, China's increasing activities have been similar to those on the Latin American mainland. Four island groups (Haiti, Saint Kitts and Nevis, Saint Lucia, and Saint Vincent and the Grenadines) continue to recognize Taiwan. Recent interest shown by Jamaica in making investments through the Belt and Road Initiative demonstrates the continuing interest in China in the area. The United States' historic dominating role in Jamaica became evident when the American ambassador sought to undermine Jamaican interest in cooperating with China, when he was quoted as saying: "I could tell you horror stories of countries where [China] has taken over ports because those countries could not pay for their investment. China usually has a great propaganda story as to why it has happened." Some ambassadors should speak less, especially when they carry a large stick.

One commentator (Scott MacDonald, *Global Americans*) on December 19, 2019, saw the America–Jamaica "tiff" over China as reflecting three major changes in the global system. These were (a) the shift away from globalization and multilateralism to economic nationalism; (b) the Caribbean reverting back to the region's historical role of being a cockpit of great power rivalries; and (c) the Caribbean countries becoming emboldened to exercise their sovereignty in terms of playing off the great powers to meet their national interests. MacDonald went on to comment that with "China's economic penetration into the Caribbean, the U.S. now has a rival for the hearts and minds of people in the region."

The United States is just as neuralgic or neurological about its neighbourhood as China. While China's activities in both Latin America and the Caribbean have been small, when compared to its activities throughout the world, the United States has been inept and insensitive to the area in both its reactions or interest in offering new ideas and policies that might be seen as helpful. The absolutism of President Trump's narrow "America first" policies and his racist comments on immigration have widened the gap between Washington and the many capitals of its southern neighbours. Unfortunately, the default in American policy remains one of making large enemies out of small countries, as is evident with Venezuela, Cuba, and Nicaragua, ensuring a welcoming field on which China can play.

Africa

A number of years ago, a provocative and sometimes perceptive Irish writer, diplomat, and politician remarked that the "future looked black" at the time the first sub-Saharan African country achieved independence. This was Ghana in 1957 with Kwame Nkrumah as prime minister. Ghana's colonial name was the "Gold Coast," illustrating the illusionary in the naming of little-known countries far from London. Conor Cruise O'Brien was the writer in question, and his perceptiveness and/or ambiguity should be questioned today, as "black" was spelled without a capital "B."

The unifying of the British colonial territories of the Gold Coast, Ashanti, the Northern Territories, and British Togoland into the Dominion of Ghana subsumed lands with a rich and ancient cultural and political heritage. Only the Ashanti in central Ghana have been able to retain some semblance of that ancient heritage. Completing the historical narrative, Prime Minister Nkrumah became president of the Republic of Ghana in 1960, and in 1966, while visiting Zhou Enlai in Beijing, he was told not to come home as a military government had been installed.

Nkrumah died in 1972 while in permanent exile, still promoting his lifelong dream of a united Africa, referred to as Pan Africanism. Time does change appreciation for historical figures—Nkrumah's remains were returned to Ghana and can now be found in a large memorial tomb in a park in Accra. He is also celebrated with a Kwame Nkrumah Memorial Day. Reflecting the outlandishness of the American government's views both at the time and today, documents were released by the Department of State describing Nkrumah as "doing more to undermine [U.S. government] interests than any other black African". The world collapses when forced into American policy preordinations.

This small bit of history illustrating the transition of some of Africa's rich cultural lands from European colonies into independent countries is only a limited view of what happened. Ghana's independence was relatively peaceful. Independence for many others involved large-scale violence, as seen in Algeria, Mozambique, Angola, Congo, and Guinea, and even greater violence over time to end apartheid in South Africa and the elimination of settler-colonial societies in Kenya and Zimbabwe. In the intervening years, there has been continuing strife, violence, and tragedy as these newly created countries sought to establish national communities out of dominated, divergent, and differing peoples.

Kwame Nkrumah being in China when the Ghanaian military told him not to come home illustrates, in part, the modern interest of African countries towards China. Yet for the Chinese, an interest and involvement in Africa predates that of Europe. Today that interest and involvement has grown and has outdistanced that from Europe and the United States. Importantly, involvement comes with greater commonality than there is with the Europeans and Americans. When African nations are referred to as "shithole countries" by the president of the United States, there is a collective shudder of unbridgeable horror. Nevertheless, altruism is a rare community in the relations between countries, and as with Europe and the United States, the interest and involvement of China is not loaded with selflessness and compassion.

Surprisingly, the African continent, consisting of some fifty-five countries, displays greater unity than any other geographically based collective of countries. The commonalities of a recent history of colonial domination, slavery, racism, and economic predation from outsiders have combined to create some measure of common purpose. Its current continent-wide organization, the African Union (AU), in its sparseness of title, gives recognition to the objective of a small group of people to recreate an Africa of significance, not only to its residents but to the hundreds of millions of African descendants living in diasporic communities created by slavery. The idea of a "return to Africa" has been experimented with but has little interest today. Instead, the people of Africa are a beacon of hope for the hundreds of millions in the diaspora where slogans such as Black Lives Matter is a rallying cry. Together, they are a harbinger of our collective new world.

Yet, Africa remains the poorest of all continents. Only Nigeria (twenty-sixth) and South Africa (thirty-sixth) are in the top fifty countries of the World Bank's compilation based on nominal GDP. Even in the list of the next fifty countries, only nine African countries appear, with five in North Africa. These are Algeria (fifty-fourth), Morocco (fifty-eighth), Ethiopia (sixty-second), Ghana (seventy-second), Ivory Coast (seventy-eighth), Libya (eighty-fourth), Democratic Republic of Congo (eighty-seventh), Tunisia (ninety-first) and Uganda (ninety-fifth).

Within the concept of African unity, there is large diversity in its political ordering. Monarchies, democracies, dictatorships, socialism, capitalism, crony capitalism, and in a few places, anarchy, all strive to create some measure of progress for the 1.3 billion people of the continent. The scope for change is evident with a median age of slightly less than twenty years, and with close to 50 percent of Africans living in an urban environment.

It is into this diversity that China today, more than any other country, has provided significant and helpful attention. China's economic ties with the continent are now vast; it is now Africa's largest trading partner, replacing the United States more than a decade ago. Over a million Chinese citizens live in Africa and there are an estimated two hundred thousand Africans working in China. To give focus to this involvement, some twenty years ago, China and nearly all African countries created the Forum on China–Africa Cooperation (FOCAC). Shortly after the formation of FOCAC, Beijing wrote that joint efforts with Africa were "to maintain the lawful rights of developing countries and push forward the creation of a new, fair and just political and economic order in the world."

A recent summation of China–Africa economic ties reported eight hundred Chinese corporations doing business in Africa, most of which are private and are investing in the infrastructure, energy, and banking sectors; there are unconditional and low-rate credit lines replacing more restricted and conditional Western loans; more than $10 billion in debt owed by African nations to China has been cancelled; one-third of China's oil supplies comes from the continent, mainly from Angola; and investments in the oil and gas exploration on the west coast of Africa have expanded. On the other hand, exports from Africa to China include 20 percent of China's cotton needs coming from Benin, Burkina Faso, and Mali; cocoa coming from the Ivory Coast; coffee coming from Kenya; and fish products coming from Namibia, its main supplier.

China has not ignored the turmoil and violence that attends some African countries. In one of the last articles published by Michael Kovrig with the International Crisis Group before he was imprisoned by Beijing in December 2018, he wrote:

> China's growing engagement with African countries got a publicity boost on 3-4 September with the latest Forum on China-Africa Cooperation (FOCAC). The triennial event brought leaders and officials from 53 African

countries and the African Union (AU) to Beijing for meetings that culminated in a resolution to continue strengthening ties and a renewed pledge of billions of dollars in Chinese loans, grants and investments. Over the past decade China's role in peace and security has also grown rapidly through arms sales, military cooperation and peacekeeping deployments in Africa. Today, through FOCAC and support to the AU and other mechanisms, China is making a growing effort to take a systematic, pan-African approach to security on the continent.

In his article of October 24, 2018, Mr. Kovrig further wrote:

This rising role in security undergirds Beijing's economic statecraft and commercial interests in Africa, helps professionalise China's military and protect its citizens there and furthers its ambitions to be a major power with global influence. The rapid pace of change is taking Chinese security policy practitioners into new territory. To avoid pitfalls for themselves and their African partners, they should deepen their expertise on local politics, societies and cultures, and the dynamics of conflict and its remedies; better monitor and modulate how China's own engagement affects stability on the continent; and work more transparently with other governments, multilateral organizations and civil society to address problems.

The complete article can be found on the International Crisis Group website.

Africa has not been hesitant in its appreciation of the benefits of its cooperation with China. Only one of the fifty-five countries of the AU (eSwatini, formerly Swaziland) still retains diplomatic relations with China. Last year in July the UN ambassadors of thirty-seven African countries signed a letter to the United Nations High Commissioner for Refugees (UNHCR) expressing support for

China's policies towards the Uyghurs and other Muslim minority groups in Xinjiang.

Middle East

The sophistication of Chinese diplomacy today is fully evident in China's approach to the countries of the Middle East. In an area where the diplomatic boats of many countries have sundered, China has been adept in developing sound and expanding relations with all of the countries in the region. In doing so, it has successfully defied the local extremities of politics, religion, and geopolitical positioning.

The reason for this large effort is not hard to find. China's growing energy need has to be satisfied as its own domestic production declines. Not so many years ago, China was self-sufficient in oil and gas, but its extraordinary economic growth in the past thirty years is built on energy, and increasingly, gas arriving in-country in a liquified form. China's energy usage accounts for 25 percent of the world's total, and oil and gas represent more than 30 percent of its complete energy demand. While it is not highlighted elsewhere in this text, a major component of China's activities in Africa, South America, and Canada relates to the country's need to import oil and gas, and there is every indication this will continue for years to come. Even in its own marine exclusive economic zone, the associated claimed areas, and the neighbouring countries in Southeast Asia, oil and gas matters constitute a major component. And it is not only the product itself; the marine and land routes for its transportation into China form a significant component of the overall foreign policy. Energy and especially oil and gas are a policy in *tous azimuts.*

In the Middle East, seven countries supply over 40 percent of China's crude oil imports, with almost one-fifth coming from Saudi Arabia, an amount worth over $40 billion in 2019. Iraq, Oman, Kuwait, the United Arab Emirates, Iran, and Libya are large suppliers as well. China's other top suppliers include Russia, Angola, Brazil, the United Kingdom, Congo, Malaysia, Colombia, and Venezuela, demonstrating the many oil barrels from which China's energy needs are met.

China has stayed aloof from various conflicts in the Middle East, both real and potential. In doing so, it has successfully played the region, country by country, expanding bilateral relations and avoiding becoming an element in the larger struggles. Thus, it has excellent relations with Israel, including trade in military equipment, which the United States has failed to curtail. Similarly, with Iran, the relationship is good. China has avoided taking sides in the Saudi–Iran contest for dominance in the Persian Gulf. Equally, China sees no need to emulate America's tendency to make large enemies out of small countries. Unlike Russia, which decided a few years ago to engage militarily in the Middle East, China has avoided any military commitments. This at a time when America's continuing interests increasingly begin and end with Israel. With the decades-long Benjamin Netanyahu extremism policy gambit coming to an end, there does not appear to be a reasonable plan by the Americans or anyone else to re-engage the Palestinians in a meaningful settlement process.

Beyond the oil, gas, and security files, China is also exploiting its recognized ability to take on large-scale infrastructure projects. Egypt has been of specific interest as the Suez Canal is of vital importance to China's inbound and export trade. As a result, billions of dollars have been invested thereto improve its domestic facilities and the development of the Red Sea port at Ain Sokhna. Illustrating the closeness of the relationship, President Abdel Fattah El-Sisi has been to Beijing six times since taking office in 2014, while Washington has only seen the president twice. Elsewhere, over two hundred thousand Chinese nationals live in the United Arab Emirates (UAE), forming an entrepot for Chinese trade, while the UAE government sees itself playing a role in the Belt and Road Initiative.

7. External Wars and Internal Conflicts

Ngaba carries the distinction of being "the undisputed world capital of self-immolations."
—Barbara Demick, 2020

Since the 1949 victory by the forces of Mao Zedong and the escape of the nationalist forces of Chiang Kai-shek to Taiwan, China has used its armed forces nine times. Four involved the settlement of internal conflicts and issues while five others involved wars with bordering countries. The internal uses—Tibet, Xinjiang, Tiananmen, Hong Kong—largely involved or involve domestic matters. The five external uses of the PLA involved the ongoing military standoff with Taiwan and the wars in North Korea, India, the Soviet Union, and Vietnam.

Early in the aftermath of the 1949 victory, there was a brief rebellion by forces in Tibet seeking independence. This failed and Tibet was formally reincorporated into China in 1950. In 1958–1959 there was a further uprising that was brutally supressed. Today there is an overwhelming process of Sinicization in Tibet, and organized Tibetan opposition is rare and ineffective. India continues to provide refuge to a large number of Tibetans as well as a home to the current Dalai Lama, and this to some extent forms part of that ongoing India–China conflict.

A recent book by Barbara Demick, *Eat the Buddha: Life and Death in a Tibetan Town* details life in the town of Ngaba, Sichuan, where some 150 Tibetans have self-immolated in recent years. Ngaba carries the distinction of being "the undisputed world capital of self-immolations." The techniques of self-immolation are chilling and reflect the desperation and tragedy of those involved. Methods include "wrapping themselves in quilts and wire to prevent rescue, dousing themselves in gasoline and swallowing it too, to ensure they will burn, from the inside."

The Tibetan diaspora is extensive, but it is out of touch with China and the Dalai Lama, who is semi-retired in India. The identification of the Dalai Lama's successor is an issue of some significance. However, the possibility of independence for Tibet is no longer a driving force. Instead, protection for the Tibetan schools of Buddhism and the Tibetan language within an autonomous region of China has emerged as the best that can be achieved. Demick reports that in Ngaba, "the last Tibetan-language school—the last one in all of China—has switched to teaching primarily in Chinese". This is physical and cultural genocide at its most basic.

Another internal conflict is ongoing. In 1960, there was an uprising in western Xinjiang province that was readily defeated, but there are continuing efforts by the people of the region for greater autonomy and religious freedom. The recent creation of "re-education" camps or prisons (depending on the observer) for Muslim Uyghurs has given the issue greater international attention than in the past. Xinjiang, in many ways, is less western China than it is east-central Asia, where Islam is completely ascendant in the bordering countries of Kazakhstan, Kyrgyzstan, Tajikistan, Afghanistan, and Pakistan. These countries have not protested Chinese actions in Xinjiang but balance the interests of their co-religious with the economic benefits of cooperating with China.

Recently, the United States decided that protesting Chinese actions in Xinjiang was of some value in its inventory of issues on which to attack China. However, in a book by a White House insider, it was reported that two years ago President Trump told President Xi building detention camps for hundreds of thousands of Muslims and other ethnic and religious minorities in western China was "exactly the right thing to do." There are no signs that international attention on Xinjiang will change the policies of Beijing in this strategically important area of China.

The events of 1989 in Tiananmen Square are known by several names. It is referred to as the Tiananmen Square Protests or

Incident or Massacre or the Six-Four Incident or the '89 Democracy Movement. The events are worthy of note for three reasons. The first was the initial indecision by the authorities in how to deal with the largely student-based protests, which began in April in Beijing. This was only thirteen years after the death of Mao and there were contending forces within the leadership. The death in early April of Hu Yaobang, the reformist general secretary of the Chinese Communist Party, initiated public manifestations by students about the course of future events and these continued for more than six weeks. The protests were large and inclusive of many who regarded the liberalization of the regime as an essential feature for reform, and a large mannequin of the Statue of Liberty was prominently displayed. Towards the end of May, the regime coalesced around the views of Deng Xiaoping that the protests were a threat to the Party and had to be ended. Martial law was declared on May 20 and upwards of three hundred thousand troops were deployed to Beijing. Two weeks later, on June 4, the troops acted and quickly put an end to the protests. The numbers of both protestors and onlookers killed are still disputed, but well over a thousand died, with some estimating up to three thousand deaths occurred.

The second element of note was the ultimate willingness of the regime to use maximum force to end the protests. While the regime initially dithered on how to handle the protests, the realization that there were increasing numbers in the streets acting in opposition to the government put an end to the indecision. The mobilization of troops from five of China's seven military districts provided the needed massive force that was used. No concessions were made to any of the demands of the protestors, which were largely political, and the shock of the regime's action put an end to such protests to this day. In the aftermath, there were widespread arrests, expulsions of foreign journalists, and a total clampdown on all information associated with the events, a clampdown that continues to the present. Importantly, it put an end to any suggestion that political reforms were part of the changes underway in China. Some have suggested that the changes then underway in Eastern Europe and the Soviet Union gave the regime the firm resolve not to allow matters to move to the point where ultimatums had to be negotiated.

China in a Changing World

The third element of note was the reaction from the international community. There were widespread condemnations from tens of countries; ambassadors were withdrawn and various embargoes, including for military equipment, were instituted. The effect of these reactions in Beijing was zero and it was not long before there was a return to the status quo ante in how the world interacted with China. It was business as usual, and competition increased from many countries to improve relations with Beijing.

The last internal issue of some consequence—and at this time, of widespread international interest—is Hong Kong. However, so far it is less of an issue for the PLA than it is one engaging greater involvement by security forces from the mainland. The needs of Beijing in the 1990s in making arrangements for the termination of the British lease for Kowloon and ending the colonial status of Hong Kong island, concluding 157yearsof British rule and making it an integral sovereign part of China, were different than they are today. During these negotiations, there was a willingness on the part of China to soften the transfer by underplaying sovereignty using the "one country, two systems" formula (OCTS) created earlier by Deng Xiaoping. This OCTS formula saw Hong Kong as a Special Administrative Region of China for some fifty years.

Twenty years after the 1997 transfer, and with President Xi firmly in control in Beijing and the Chinese economy having a life of its own, the opportunity to revisit the gift of the special status for Hong Kong was at hand. The area's economic importance had lessened and the last vestige of colonialism it represented was irritating to many. Coincidentally, large numbers of people in Hong Kong have come to appreciate the value of what was arranged in 1997 and decided this was worth maintaining. Even the word "independence" was heard from time to time, and if there was ever a situation of the "red cloth" enraging a bull, that was it for the hard men in power in Beijing.

The new security law imposed on Hong Kong by Beijing does not alter completely some of the important features of Hong Kong's Basic Law. There is still overt recognition of the capitalistic economic system with its own currency, along with a basic but limited representative system of government. The "representative" system of government, ironically, was largely initiated by the British in its last three years of rule. The legal system, so far, remains similar to that in Canada and the United Kingdom, and many of the same rights and freedoms exist. But with the abruptness of the imposition of the new security law giving Beijing control over broadly defined areas of subversion, secession, terrorism, and collusion with foreigners, there are legitimate concerns around Beijing's ultimate objectives. It is entirely possible there will be early termination of the fifty-year lifespan of the "one country, two systems" arrangement.

The early reaction of some Western countries to these early changes in Hong Kong's status suggest to some they are part of the changing attitudes towards China. If so, then there is little likelihood they will change much in the policies and actions of Beijing. Also, in their negativity, we are undermining the possibility of developing a more sophisticated approach in dealing with the new China. As such, it limits the possibility of effectively providing help to those directly affected. So far, the range of measures announced by some countries (financial measures and visa restrictions against specific officials, cancellation of extradition treaties, possible easier visa arrangements for the citizens of Hong Kong) do not amount to much and will not cause deep concern for Beijing.

This is not the Beijing of 1989, nor do President Xi and his supporters have an interest in causing self-imposed harm to the Chinese economy, even if that is only a distant prospect. Equally, it can be assumed that Beijing leaders have taken a close measure of the world around them and have concluded there is not much to fear in retaliatory measures for its actions on Hong Kong. With elections due in a COVID-19 ravaged and ideologically divisive United States, and Europe still recovering from the pandemic, retaliatory measures will be more verbal than seriously economic. In the United States, Biden and Trump are already exchanging empty salvos on who has been softer on China. It will be a small opera for the stage in the years to come.

China in a Changing World

External Wars

Taiwan. The escape of Nationalist forces to Taiwan in 1949 at the end of the civil war on the mainland prompted policies and actions by Beijing aimed at forcing reincorporation of the island into China. In the 1950s and 1960s, there were artillery exchanges between the two forces across the Taiwan Strait and threatening troop deployments on the mainland. Today, the conflict has become one more of words and international positioning than overt military action. Economically, Taiwan and the mainland have created a cooperative relationship.

Another factor of significance for the coming years is the possibility Taiwan will declare itself an independent country and seek international support. There is significant support for such a move in Taiwan but it has remained a tantalizing idea rather than a defined plan for the future. Beijing would see the move as crossing an important divide, and in retaliation would unleash actions up to and including large-scale military operations. In large measure and until the recent emergence of a reasonably democratic political system on the island, the government in Taiwan maintained the fiction that it was the government of all China. The essential feature of this reflected the unity of China and was and is a fiction that Beijing could live with. To move away from that fiction would totally undermine the fragile understandings that have guided Beijing–Taipei relations since 1949.

It cannot be assumed the relatively benign relationship between Beijing and Taipei today will remain the norm in the years ahead. There has been some measure of caution in both capitals in the various bilateral efforts made to provide complementary benefits. The economic relationship has grown over the years and is today one of significant value to both countries. Equally, the slow erosion of the number of countries recognizing Taiwan as the "Republic of China" makes that issue meaningless. The relative calm and the continuing cheque-writing effort by Beijing will see the disappearance of diplomatic recognition of Taiwan by the remaining thirteen countries. Even Beijing and the Vatican have been discussing measures on recognition for some time.

Two factors could undermine the relative normalcy of Taiwan–Beijing relations. The first is whether the increasingly hard line by Beijing in dealing with the world will extend to Taiwan. It remains as the single historical anomaly in the emergence of China as a global power. It is not unusual for the over-confident to try and eliminate such a large anomaly, and there is an overabundance of confidence in Beijing at this time.

The second factor would be the role of the United States in the months ahead as it adjusts for its diminishing role in world affairs. There is a growing sense in the United States that its problems are not of its own making, but that the efforts of others, including China, are responsible. As such, it is most likely that Taiwan could emerge as the one place where military confrontation could take place in the years ahead.

North Korea. China's land borders contain and retain elements for future conflicts. Its million-man intervention in 1950 in Korea, countering the deep incursion of UN forces into North Korea that neared the Chinese border, eventually led to a stalemate and the establishment of the demilitarized zone (DMZ) between North and South Korea that still stands today. The creation of North Korea provided China with a large physical buffer zone with American forces in South Korea. It is a buffer zone of significance to Beijing and one that it will work at maintaining. Despite the often troublesome relationship with North Korea, China will ensure the continued protection and continuation of the North Korean regime, and, as in 1950, China would be willing to deploy its military forces in support of that effort. At the time, for the newly created United Nations and especially the role of United States, Korea was the first of America's postwar defeats and the creation of the sad commentary by those involved "to die for a tie."

India. The Sino–Indian War in 1962 was largely caused by foolhardy Indian efforts to extend and/or maintain boundaries established by the British decades earlier. The Jawaharlal Nehru and V. K. Krishna Menon leadership was particularly inept in its expectation that the spirit of Bandung would protect it from Chinese reaction. Reality struck when the Chinese army was on its way to Calcutta, and there were hurried efforts for a ceasefire. However, the border with India both north of Calcutta and in the west involving Aksai Chin remains largely unmarked and unsettled.

The Aksai Chin border, in the Indian state of Ladakh and southwestern Tibet, has seen skirmishes in the past weeks and military commanders in the area have been meeting to defuse the clashes. China took control of the area in the 1962 war and, at 14,000 feet, it made for the highest battlefield in the world. India reported the death of twenty soldiers in mid-June 2020 clashes and the capture of an unstated number. China appears to have occupied land on the Indian side of the line of control, but this is unverified. The clashes were significant despite the fact that no shots were fired. Both sides used rocks, wooden clubs, and hand-to-hand combat. China has not yet reported any deaths.

The area borders the Siachen Glacier, which is an area of ongoing dispute between India and Pakistan. India took control of the glacier in 1984 and there were clashes with Pakistan for a number of years, though it has been relatively quiet in the last decade. Pakistan contends that the glacier area is an extension of the line of control separating Pakistani-administered Kashmir and Indian-administered Kashmir. China regards the area of some importance in its expanding Belt and Road Initiative. Roads through the area, as well as in Aksai Chin, have economic, military, and strategic value.

The eight-hundred-mile Karakoram Highway, running from the northwestern Indian Ocean near the Pakistani border with Iran into the Chinese city of Kashgar, is to the north of these conflict areas. This highway threads a needle between these areas of dispute, and the borders with Afghanistan and Tajikistan. The terrain makes it unlikely that large-scale military conflict is either possible or wanted by any of the contending countries. Nevertheless, the history of the area and the interests of the parties involved will not produce any willingness for an early settlement of the conflicting issues and claims.

India and China have each made efforts to establish a reasonable relationship in recent years. However, China's economic assertiveness throughout the Indian Ocean basin, along with the establishment of Chinese-financed port facilities in Myanmar, Sri Lanka, Pakistan, and Djibouti, creates large uncertainties for New Delhi. In large part, this has created an increasingly close relationship between India and the United States. It is the best now that it has been since Indian independence in 1947. In many ways, some consider India as a counterweight to Chinese expansion in the area. Yet, so far there are few signs that India, in its policies and actions, would be very effective as a significant player in any larger effort to moderate the expansionist and dominating policies of Beijing.

Russia. China and the Soviet Union went to war in 1969 along the northern border of Xinjian on the Ussuri River. The war, in part, reflected the Sino–Soviet ideological split of the time associated with the 1968 Soviet invasion of Czechoslovakia. A series of border agreements beginning in the early 1990s have largely settled the issues involved. However, there are lingering fears in Russia of Chinese territorial ambitions in Siberia, which Mao at one point claimed were once part of China. In the foreseeable future, there is a commonality of interests, especially in countering the actions of the United States in the region and elsewhere.

Vietnam. In present-day terms, the decades-long military war and skirmishing beginning in 1979 between China and Vietnam is the most consequential. China occupied several areas in northern Vietnam that were returned in a 1992 agreement. Of greatest consequence was the realization by Beijing that the People's Liberation Army had serious deficiencies as the Vietnamese more than held their own in some of the pitched battles. This led to a large-scale and ongoing modernization of China's armed forces, with most observers suggesting that it is today a very able and modern fighting force. Its air force and navy elements have modernized to the point that they are close to challenging those available to the United States in the region. Its space program is well-financed and growing. As part of the war with Vietnam, China also occupied and took control of reefs associated with the Spratly Islands in the South China Sea.

8. Stormy Seas

> *Long before European countries began their open seas exploratory voyages, China was building large ships and trading with countries of the Indian Ocean and the western Pacific. Unlike European policies in later years, China did not "claim" these lands; instead, they were seen in terms of their economic value to China.*

Beyond land border issues, China's activities in nearly all of the seas of the world have also created interest and concern. In particular, its activities in the East and South China Seas are seen by many, in the region and beyond, as the most consequential and troublesome.

China, like the United States, is a party of the United Nations Convention on the Law of the Sea (UNCLOS), though neither has ratified and both use its provisions in the promotion of marine activities when appropriate. A strong element in China's approach is to avoid international adjudication of marine disputes, preferring instead bilateral negotiations with disputing countries. China intends to militarily dominate its contiguous marine areas and see the exclusion of other powers, especially the United States.

The activities associated with China's Belt and Road Initiative (BRI), announced in May 2017, economically connecting China to the countries of Oceania, Asia, Europe, and Africa, are tied to its domination of its neighbouring seas and presence elsewhere. So far

China is involved in forty-two port projects in thirty-four countries largely associated with the BRI. While most are of mutual economic value, some provide a possible strategic military advantage that could support Chinese naval operations in many parts of the world. Three of these ports are in the Indian Ocean, in Pakistan, Myanmar, and Sri Lanka; a fourth is nearby in Cambodia, and a fifth is in Djibouti in northeast Africa.

China is not generally regarded as a maritime power. This is a serious misunderstanding. Long before European countries began their open seas exploratory voyages, China was building large ships and trading with countries in the Indian Ocean and the western Pacific. Unlike European policies in later years, China did not "claim" these lands; instead, they were seen in terms of their economic value to China.

The seven voyages between 1403 and 1433 to East Africa and Arabia led by Admiral Zheng He are the best known, and provide historical context for present-day Chinese marine intentions. There is conflicting information on the size of the ships of this period, but they were larger than those of other countries. They did include one significant technological feature: their internal compartmentation, which was later adopted by other shipbuilders.

China has also been active in Arctic matters. China has held official observer status on the Arctic Council since 2013, identifying itself as a "near Arctic state." In public announcements, China considers the Arctic to be part of the world's "common heritage," and has not objected to the application of UNCLOS Exclusive Economic Zone provisions to the region.

In 2012, the Chinese icebreaker *Xue Long* sailed the Northeast Passage ("the Ice Road"). Since then, there have been numerous transits by freighters taking advantage of the fact that shipping from Shanghai to Hamburg is four thousand miles shorter than through the Suez Canal. China is building a second icebreaker and has announced plans for a nuclear-powered vessel in the coming year. Chinese ships have sailed through the Northwest Passage as well, but China has not expressed views on Canada's claim that the passage is part of its internal waters.

China is also the most important fishing nation on the planet. It is estimated that China has almost seventeen thousand deep-water fishing vessels, which has significant effects on the environment and socioeconomic impacts on developing countries. In a recent article (2019) in *The Maritime Executive*, independent fisheries expert Gilles Hosch writes that China confers "its flag to a vast fleet of thousands of fishing vessels and fish carriers, operating not just within the Chinese exclusive economic zone (EEZ) but across all major ocean basins. China is also one of the three most important global seafood markets, ranking as the top seafood exporter and third-largest importer."

In an index developed by Poseidon Aquatic Resource Management in Geneva, countries are compared according to their illegal, unreported, and unregulated (IUU) fishing worldwide. Hosch reports that the index "reveals that China faces its most formidable challenges as a flag and a port state, where it ranks as the worst performer globally. Its ranks in the coastal state and general group of responsibilities are marginally better (13th and fourth respectively)." Notably, the performance of most coastal countries leaves considerable room for improvement. Yet, for China, there is a need for action given the scope of its activities and the significance of fish in its culture and economy.

Ecuador was the most recent country to see a massive Chinese fishing fleet arrive in its neighbourhood. In late July 2020, an estimated 260 Chinese-flagged fishing vessels arrived off the Galapagos Islands. In 2017, a similar fleet was in the same waters and there were reports of illegal fishing, but it appears there was little that could be done to curtail the fishing by this fleet as it largely operated on the high seas. One vessel was caught in the nearby Galapagos Marine Reserve with three hundred tons of sharks. The Ecuadorian authorities are seeking international assistance in curtailing such activities, but so far there appears to be little help on offer.

It is, however, China's marine boundaries involving three neighbouring seas that are of immediate and particular concern: the Yellow Sea involving both Koreas; the East China Sea involving disputes with Taiwan, South Korea, and Japan; and the South China Sea involving disputes with Brunei, Indonesia, Malaysia, the Philippines, Taiwan, and Vietnam.

Nearly 40 percent of world trade travels through these waters and freedom of navigation is central to all of these disputes. Importantly, the United States maintains the right for its naval and air force units to operate in international waters in these seas without prior permission, control, or hindrance. These disputes also involve the sharing of large potential and/or actual oil and gas underwater reserves. As with all large bodies of water, fishing rights also result in daily friction, if not physical conflict.

The Sea of Japan. The Sea of Japan (also known as the East Sea of Korea in North Korea and East Sea in South Korea) separates the islands of the Japanese archipelago, Russia's Sakhalin Island, the Russian mainland, and the Korean Peninsula. There are disputes involving small islands between North and South Korea and Japan. North Korea and Russia have an agreement for their overlapping Exclusive Economic Zones, but the status of the overlapping zones between the Koreas and Japan is unclear. As well, Japan regularly protests the use of the air over the Sea of Japan for missile testing by North Korea. The historical dispute over the naming of this sea also continues, and it is expected that the International Hydrographic Organization will report on the matter in the coming months. There are no disputes directly involving China.

The Yellow Sea. The Yellow Sea (known as the West Sea in the Koreas) is the exception, in that there are no marine boundary disputes involving China. However, the western end of the North and South Korean demarcation line extends into this sea, and this has occasioned naval confrontations. In late 2018, a buffer zone was created, although few expect the area will be free of future confrontations between the Koreas. The Yellow Sea is badly overfished by the Koreas, China, and Japan.

East China Sea. Disputes in the East China Sea involve the application of the two-hundred-mile Exclusive Economic Zones (EEZ) of UNCLOS, and mainly involve Japan. This sea is only 360 miles in width, ending with the Japanese Ryukyu Islands, inclusive of Okinawa. As such, there is less water to divide relative to the EEZ standard of two hundred miles. China argues the divide should take into account the provisions of the continental shelf articles of the UNCLOS in the area, and as such, extend its EEZ beyond the standard two hundred miles. Japan has proposed a median line demarcation. The matter is before UNCLOS, but it is not expected to rule for several years. The dispute with South Korea involves the underwater Socotra Rock (a sea mount),where South Korea has constructed a marine research station. China argues that this is in violation of its EEZ rights in the area. There is some confusion as to whether the sea mount is in the Yellow Sea or the East China Sea.

In late 2013, China established an Air Defense Identification Zone (ADIZ) in the East China Sea. Such zones are relatively common, with more than twenty countries, including Canada, the United States, Japan, and Taiwan having established them. However, they are not defined in any treaty nor regulated by any international organization with appropriate responsibility. China's establishment of this zone was criticized by most of its neighbours, the European Union, and the United States on the basis that it covered disputed territory and the ADIZ overlaps with zones already established by other countries in the region. It also imposes reporting requirements for both military and civilian aircraft. Most of the civilian aircraft travelling in the area report their presence. It is unclear if aircraft from Japan report their presence to China, and it is equally unclear if military aircraft flying in the area report to China. There have been press reports that American military aircraft do not report. In 2014, China announced that it was not considering the establishment of a zone over the South China Sea.

South China Sea. In the South China Sea, there exists a Gordian knot of conflicting claims, counterclaims, navigation rights, fishing rights, national status, and territoriality without easy or early solutions available. Most of the countries involved prefer international arbitration rather than bilateral negotiations with China to resolve these disputes.

Chinese claims in this sea involve the use of a unique feature in maritime law: the "dash-line." The line finds reflection in recent Chinese history just prior to the revolution, and over time has had eleven, nine, and ten "dashes" associated with it in support of claims in the South China Sea. Today there are ten "dashes," with one east of Taiwan, and as such, it is not part of the South China Sea claims. The "nine-dash line" partially reflects and/or supports China's "historic use" claims involving the Paracel Islands (two hundred miles from Hainan Island, where there is a Chinese nuclear submarine base), the Spratly and Pratas islands, as well as the Macclesfield Bank and the Scarborough Shoal (220 miles from Manila). These claims are in conflict with one or more of the claims of Brunei, Indonesia, Malaysia, the Philippines, and Vietnam. The Republic of China (Taiwan) in public statements generally has claims similar to those of China and generally supports China's claims.

Associated with its claims in the South China Sea, China has constructed and continues to construct military, dual use, and civilian facilities on the sea's islands, shoals, and artificial reefs. These facilities, generally, are considered defensive (except perhaps any that might be created on the Scarborough Shoal), and create, in the view of China, de facto Chinese sovereignty over large areas of the sea. Such a view does not find reflection or support in the UNCLOS. The installations include harbours, runways, helipads, aircraft storage buildings, radar facilities, ground-to-air missile systems, troop garrison facilities, lighthouses, bunkers, and signals intelligence facilities. There are civilian facilities on Woody Island of the Paracel group, designated as the official administrative headquarters for the islands claimed by China as its territory, which include the Paracels and Spratly Islands, and the Scarborough Shoal. There are civilian air connections with Woody Island from the mainland.

There are also conflicting claims with five neighbouring countries. None have accepted China's claims using the nine-dash line, and they maintain that it is contrary to the provisions of the UNCLOS. An international arbitration tribunal established under Article VII of UNCLOS at the request of the Philippines considered Chinese claims on the Scarborough Shoal. The tribunal ruled in 2016 there was "no legal basis for China to claim historic rights" relating to the nine-dash line. The tribunal also ruled that China had violated the Philippines' sovereign rights and caused "severe harm to the coral reef environment." China did not participate in the tribunal and called the decision "ill-founded." Taiwan, which administers Taiping Island of the Spratly group, also rejected the ruling by the tribunal.

This ruling by the tribunal provided some measure of encouragement and support for the countering claims by the five neighbouring countries. But it does not and will not put an end to China's claim, and most likely the issue will have to be settled by bilateral and/or regional negotiations. All of the five neighbouring countries are seriously outgunned by China, and already there are signs that not all will want to prolong the disputes should there be serious economic consequences imposed by Beijing.

The Philippines in particular, under President Rodrigo Duterte, has been diffident, if not erratic, in its dealings with Beijing on the possibility of Chinese activities on the Scarborough Shoal. Only Vietnam is likely to remain confrontational with Beijing, reflecting that some of the Spratly Islands were part of Vietnam but were occupied by China in the 1989 war and not relinquished. The other countries—Brunei, Indonesia, and Malaysia—will carefully measure the economic cost of opposing China with its countering claims. There are ongoing skirmishes, but these relate to fishing rights throughout the area rather than the fundamentals of the Chinese territorial claims.

The Merchant Fleet. As with all things in modern China, the life and death of Mao Zedong dominates. His long life both before and after the successful revolution in 1949 created a country of coherence and unity, mirroring large parts of its ancient history. His death in 1976 provided the point of departure for others, especially Deng Xiaoping, and today, Xi Jinping, to create the China that now dominates global affairs. The economic transformation has already been documented, and it is a consequence of that transformation that world trade increasingly carries the goods of China in ships flagged by China. There should be no great surprise in this. All of the world's large exporting countries have floated their dominance on vessels flagged at home or with the flags of several countries where "convenience" is offered and responsibility is moderated.

The uniqueness of China's merchant fleet is in the speed at which it developed and the scope of its operations. It was not until 1960 that China established its own maritime shipping firm, and by 2014, an official government document declared that a maritime shipping industry was an "important basic industry for economic and social development." One document titled "Opinion of the State Council on Promoting the Sound Development of the Shipping Industry" went on to describe a variety of reforms and reported that China ranked fourth among the world's shipping industries. The picture at that time had the industry carrying 142 million in deadweight tons, some 8 percent of the world's total, distributed among 240 shipping companies, but carrying only 25 percent of China's exports and imports.

Since then, the growth of China's merchant fleet has been described as "phenomenal," and in a paper presented at the CNA conference in 2015 in Arlington, Virginia, Dennis J. Blasko concluded that the number of ships owned by and registered in China and Hong Kong was first in the world. Since those conclusions were reached in 2015, China's dominance in global maritime shipping has continued to grow, and today it is the second-largest ship-owning country in the world. It is second to Greece, another "great" seafaring nation, and just ahead of Japan.

At one level there is nothing particularly worrisome in this, as it reflects a global economic reality. But as with all countries, a merchant marine is a significant element in their overall military structure, and in that China is no different. In the May 2015 white paper on military strategy released by the State Council Information Office of the People's Republic of China, the Chinese Ministry of National Defense wrote:

> The seas and oceans bear on the enduring peace, lasting stability and sustainable development of China. The traditional mentality that land outweighs sea must be abandoned, and great importance has to be attached to managing the seas and oceans and protecting maritime rights and interests. It is necessary for China to develop a modern maritime military force structure commensurate with its national security and development interests, safeguard its national sovereignty and maritime rights and interests, protect the security of strategic SLOCs [sea lines of communications] and overseas interests, and participate in international maritime cooperation, so as to provide strategic support for building itself into a maritime power.

9. Banks – More Than Money

> *The owners, originally from China, form part of what is now an extensive and nebulous economic network informally called the "bamboo network."*

In July 2020, there was controversy when the banking arrangements of the Canadian foreign minister were publicized. In an earlier life, before he entered politics and was living in London, the minister arranged for the financing of two properties with a bank owned by the government of the People's Republic of China. When he was named minister, the financing arrangement was disclosed to the appropriate authorities. Nevertheless, the arrangement, when publicized, suggested to some that this could lead to undue influence on the foreign minister, especially as he was dealing with China on the imprisonment of Canadians. Associated with two cases was the possible extradition of a senior Chinese business person to the United States. The minister quickly made other financing arrangements for his London properties.

In the larger scheme, the financing of properties in London for purchase by a Canadian through a state bank of China is not particularly important and probably not unique. What is important is the light it sheds on the ubiquity of Chinese financial services throughout the world, and its importance to the worldwide ambitions of China and the economic well-being of the countries involved. There are major stories daily on the creation of new companies, the purchase of existing companies, or other investments made by China throughout the world. Banking is central to all such transactions.

The scope and frequency are such that there are increasing concerns and barriers to these activities by certain countries. Existing or new national standards and controls are being enforced. In doing so, there is both unease and hope. First, the involvement of Chinese financing, for some, suggests possible future actions that may not be in the interest of the country or company concerned. Second, there is hope that the involvement may create increased economic benefit, or in some cases, the survival of a company or industry. Both issues were well illustrated a few years ago by a Chinese company's purchase of controlling interest in the iconic Swedish Volvo company. The company was in significant financial difficulty and an investment from China, at the time, was seen by all as a mutually beneficial arrangement. However, today there is considerable concern that some or all of the Volvo production facilities in Sweden could be transferred to China, where costs are considerably less.

In addition to these "retail" banking and investment facilities, China has created large financial funds to support many of its initiatives throughout the world. These include the Asian Infrastructure Investment Bank and the Silk Road Fund. This fund is tied specifically to financing projects created through the Belt and Road Initiative. As well, there is the "bamboo network," informal financing arrangements made by overseas Chinese migrants; and the Asian Development Bank, the traditional development bank modelled on the World Bank.

Bamboo Network. Sixty-five years ago, a restaurant opened in Gander, Newfoundland, and introduced moo shu pork to its customers. The restaurant, named "The Highlight," was owned by the brothers Norm and Henry Tom, and still exists. The owners, originally from China, form part of what is now an extensive and nebulous economic network informally called the "bamboo network." The network has been described as the informal connections between businesses owned and operated by overseas Chinese citizens. As we enjoyed our first moo shu pork in 1956, there was little knowledge or interest in this worldwide network, but for many before and since, it has become a useful shorthand for an "economic elite" that, in the view of one writer, forms an "extended international economic outpost of Mainland China." Maybe or not.

Historically, the network emerged in Southeast Asia, where it linked overseas Chinese businesses in Myanmar, Malaysia, Indonesia, Thailand, Vietnam, the Philippines, and Singapore. In more recent years, it became the "source" of large investment for China. The overseas Chinese business community is large, and it is courted and valued for its importance nationally and internationally. But the evidence supporting some sort of unity is more anecdotal than documentary. Equally, the idea that this community might represent an element in China's policies today is the feverish imagination of national security officials at work.

Asian Infrastructure Investment Bank (AIIB). Far removed in time and structure from the bamboo network is the Asian Infrastructure Investment Bank. Created by the government of China, it came into existence in January 2016 as both a rival and possibly a successor to the work of the World Bank, the International Monetary Fund (IMF), and the Asian Development Bank in the Asia-Pacific Region. In promoting the idea in 2015, President Xi Jinping stated, "The Chinese economy is deeply integrated with the global economy and forms an important driving force of the economy of Asia and even the world at large." The AIIB is also seen as part of the effort by Beijing to increase its prominence in Asian investment while diminishing that of the United States and Japan as they dominate decisions within the World Bank, the IMF, and the Asian Development Bank. The starting capital was $100 billion. The United States opposed its creation but the Bank has since attracted members globally and now has one hundred members. Canada became a member two years ago.

The AIIB describes itself as a "lean, clean, green" and concentrates on "sustainable infrastructure, cross-country connectivity and the mobilization of private capital." It has announced financing for over $12 billion in nearly all of the countries of Asia and beyond (Turkey, Egypt, Oman, and Azerbaijan). The AIIB has co-financed projects with the World Bank and the Asian Development Bank.

The AIIB has also become, in a very short period, a major institution in infrastructure investment despite continued American opposition. The leader of the opposition in the Canadian parliament has suggested that Canada cancel its investment in the AIIB as retaliation for actions by the government of China on such matters as a boycott of Canadian agricultural imports, and the imprisonment of two Canadians in retaliation for the arrest of prominent Chinese business person Meng Wanzhou in Vancouver. The Canadian government has given no indication that it intends to cancel its investment in the bank.

The Silk Road Fund. The Silk Road Fund was established as a state-owned institution to support financing for projects in connection with China's Belt and Road Initiative. It was established in late 2014 and had initial capitalization of $40 billion. So far it has announced financing for projects in Kenya, Pakistan, Dubai, and Russia in excess of $6 billion.

Asian Development Bank (ADB). The ADB was created in 1966, largely as a result of promotion by Japan, and is headquartered in Manila. It reflects the World Bank in operations and uses a similar weighted vote system where decisions are based on members' capital subscriptions. Japan and the United States dominate its decision making. Every president of the ADB since its creation has been Japanese. China, while a member and a borrower, has limited influence in the decisions. In large part, this lack of influence in the ADB contributed to the creation of the AIIB by China in 2016. Taiwan is a member (as Taipei, China), as is Canada.

10. Regional Organizations – Collective Comfort for the Neighbours

> *These organizations do not prevent conflict but they accentuate, create, and moderate views on matters of common interest.*

There are numerous inter- and non-governmental organizations in Asia providing an opportunity for countries in the region to cooperate and coordinate on the full range of political and economic issues. They are geographical and functional in membership and purpose, but provide for limited participation from outside the region. These organizations do not prevent conflict but they do accentuate, create, and moderate views on matters of common interest. The most important of these organizations include the Association of Southeast Asian Nations (ASEAN), the South Asian Association for Regional Cooperation (SAARC), the Pacific Islands Forum (PIF), the Asia-Pacific Economic Cooperation (APEC),the Pacific Economic Cooperation Council (PECC), and the Asia Pacific Foundation of Canada.

Association of Southeast Asian Nations (ASEAN). The countries of southeast Asia were the first to see value in creating a forum for discussion of mutual and conflicting problems. Its beginning dates back to the early 1960s, with the association being formalized in 1967. Initially, it had five member countries, Indonesia, Malaysia, the Philippines, Singapore, and Thailand, but in succeeding years, Brunei, Cambodia, Laos, Myanmar, and Vietnam became members. Papua New Guinea and East Timor have observer status. Its headquarters is in Jakarta.

In its creation, ASEAN declared its objective was to accelerate economic growth, social progress, and cultural development in the region, and to promote regional peace, collaboration, and mutual assistance on matters of common interest. Of particular note is that the association members have been prepared to take on large political issues such as the Vietnamese invasion of Cambodia in 1975. More than a decade ago, member states agreed on a charter that called for "an EU-style community" with common free trade arrangements among members, and between members and other countries.

The association has also established common standards for issues dealing with the environment and human rights, and negotiated a treaty establishing a nuclear-free zone for the ASEAN region. Member countries emphasize consultation and consensus in decision making and it has been described as "a working process or style that is informal and personal. Policymakers constantly utilize compromise, consensus and consultation in the informal decision-making process [. . .] it above all prioritizes a consensus based, non-conflictual way of addressing problems. Quiet diplomacy allows ASEAN leaders to communicate without bringing the discussions into the public view. Members avoid embarrassment that may lead to further conflict."

Since its inception, ASEAN has reached out to other interested countries seeking to establish cooperative political and economic arrangements. These include Korea, Japan, China, Australia, New Zealand, Canada, the European Union, and the United States. It has annual formal meetings with all involved countries and today there are numerous agreements and free trade arrangements in place. There are now free trade agreements with Australia, New Zealand, India, Japan, South Korea, and China.

South Asian Association for Regional Cooperation (SAARC). This South Asia-centred organization emerged in the early 1980s when there was relative peace in the region. It was influenced by the success of ASEAN in neighbouring countries. While India and Pakistan were still squabbling over Kashmir, and Sri Lanka was fighting a renewed insurgency by the Tamils, there was a significant interest in providing greater cooperation throughout the region. In the words of the time, "SAARC provides a platform for the peoples of South Asia to work together in a spirit of friendship, trust and understanding."

The headquarters for the organization is in Kathmandu and initial membership included Bangladesh, Bhutan, India, Maldives, Nepal, Pakistan, and Sri Lanka. Afghanistan became a member some twenty years after. The continuing dispute between India and Pakistan over Kashmir remains a dominating issue and it has limited the effectiveness of the organization. Until that issue is resolved to the satisfaction of both countries, it is unlikely that the organization will ever become a force for improving the quality of life for the peoples of South Asia through "accelerated economic growth, social progress and cultural development." China has developed excellent relations with all of the members except India.

Pacific Islands Forum (PIF). The forum originated as the South Pacific Forum in 1971 and is headquartered in Suva, Fiji. It has eighteen member countries and a number of observers from the American territories in the north and south Pacific. It includes both Australia and New Zealand. The American territories of American Samoa, Guam, and the Northern Mariana Islands were granted observer status in 2011, while in 2016,the French territories of French Polynesia and New Caledonia were granted full membership. There are "dialogue partnerships" with countries beyond the region; these include China, the United States, Japan, South Korea, Thailand, the Philippines, Canada, and the European Union. In the words of the forum, it works "to enhance the economic and social well-being of the people of the South Pacific by fostering cooperation between governments and between international agencies, and by representing the interests of Forum members in ways agreed by the Forum."

China has been active throughout the region with economic development projects and generally has good relations with most of the islands. Not surprisingly, there are often disputes around fishing in the economic zones of many of islands and such disputes will continue.

Asia-Pacific Economic Cooperation (APEC). APEC was formed in 1989 following the success of the ASEAN Post Ministerial Conferences of members and dialogue partners. It is headquartered in Singapore and consists of twenty-one members inclusive of both China and Taiwan (as Chinese Taipei). Hong Kong, which became a member before reversion to Chinese sovereignty in 1997, has retained its membership. There are three official observers: ASEAN, PIF, and PECC. A number of other countries have sought membership, including India, which has its own ocean, but that application and several others have been deferred. India was offered observer status.

The interest in becoming members of APEC speaks to the group's pre-eminence among such organizations. Its annual heads of government meeting, rotating among the member countries, has become a mainstay of high-level economic global management. Its main objective is to create conditions for free and open trade and investment in the Asia-Pacific region, a task that is still underway.

Pacific Economic Cooperation Council (PECC). The council was established in 1980 as an initiative by the prime ministers of Japan and Australia, and today has twenty-three full-time members, all situated around the eastern and western Pacific. It is headquartered in Singapore. China, Taiwan, and Hong Kong are members, and others include Canada, Australia, Chile, Colombia, South Korea, Mexico, United States, the Pacific Islands Forum, and Vietnam. It is a non-governmental organization, but its activities include representatives from governments. The council brings together business leaders and academics to explore, discuss, and create ideas for cooperation across the Asia-Pacific region. Its annual general meetings take place throughout the region and generally focus on the host country's involvement in matters affecting the Asia-Pacific region. Canadian involvement is organized through the Asia-Pacific Foundation headquartered in Vancouver.

Asia Pacific Foundation of Canada. The foundation was created by an Act of Parliament in 1984, and while independent, it is largely funded by the Canadian federal and provincial governments. It was created in the last days of the Pierre Elliott Trudeau government, but its creation and promotion was endorsed by the successor Progressive Conservatives under Brian Mulroney. Joe Clarke, the initial foreign minister for the Mulroney government, was a strong promoter of the foundation and Canada's relationship with countries in the Asia-Pacific region. The foundation is a leader in research and analysis on Canadian relations with Asia and offers governments policy advice and guidance on relations with Asian-Pacific countries.

11. Stumbling Americans and Wandering Russians – Recovery or Decay

> *Most relevant to the use of "empire" as a concept today are the activities of the United States and China. For the United States the "fall of empire" is the organizing concept, while for China it is "the creation of empire."*

The concept of "empire" has been a useful political construct in organizing and understanding the phantasmagorical history of the world. Despite the lack of any intellectual uniformity in the meaning and use of the concept, it remains somewhat valid in reducing the complexities of our respective histories to a common level. European colonial activities spanned the globe, and the control exercised by the British, French, Spanish, Portuguese, Dutch, and to a lesser extent, the Belgians, Germans, and Italians gave rise to the extensive use of the "empire" concept. In Asia, Japan's aggressive activities from the late-nineteenth century to 1945 mirrored those of the European powers. In part, the use of the word was self-aggrandizement, but for many it accurately reflected the power relationship between the metropolitan powers and large areas of Africa, Asia, Central and South America, the Caribbean, and the Middle East.

Today, "empire" means little as a concept in understanding the relationships and influences that underpin American global activities throughout the world. The same can be said for Russia, and in recent years, for China. The British creation of the Commonwealth of Nations provided an illusion of influence among the countries under its former domination, but this has all but disappeared. The idiocy of its decision to withdraw from the European community in 2016 ensures the death knell of any continuing global aspirations. Much the same can be said for France, Spain, and Portugal, as they seek to influence other countries through the commonality of language.

Russia's international activities fall somewhat within the classical concept of empire. Its global reach has eroded with the loss of control over several contiguous countries and the bankruptcy of the idea of "world revolution" based on the writings of nineteenth-century myopic philosophers. However, the exploitation of digital communications technologies, nuclear weapons, and UN Security Council permanent veto status provide it with some influence. Most recently, its decision to intervene militarily in Syria and Libya gave rise to concerns that new power-based relationships were underway.

Most relevant to the use of "empire" as a concept today are the activities of the United States and China. For the United States, the "fall of empire" is the organizing concept, while for China it is "the creation of empire," or perhaps "re-creation," given its long history as the major power of Asia. In both cases, the central factors in providing understanding are the unity of policy and coherence of the country. The history of China–United States relations is more complex and more egregious than most. Misunderstandings, deliberate falsifications, arrogance, faked bonhomie, and vanity have all combined to make the recent short period of bilateral reasonableness and cooperation appear as a distant age. The coming years, characterized by Chinese assertiveness and America's increasing impotence, will create a potentially serious rupture in global politics.

In China, unity of policy and coherence of country is a given and will not change significantly in the near years. In the United States, the opposite is true. The failed years of war and engagement in Afghanistan and the Middle East, and mind-shattering changes in ideology and personal values in leadership, have distorted American interests everywhere to the point where long-standing allies question the reliability and honesty of American support.

President Obama and his administration gave some recognition of this in their 2012 "pivot to East Asia," which built on policies, actions, and initiatives by presidents Bill Clinton and George W. Bush to redress the imbalances and increase American force levels in the region. Additional weapon systems were deployed to existing bases, an aircraft carrier base was established in Singapore, and the deployment of submarines to the Pacific was increased. Military ties with Australia, the Philippines, Vietnam, and India were improved, and this increased confidence in American military support in Japan and South Korea.

Acknowledging that American force levels were only one aspect of the problem, Obama initiated negotiations with eleven Pacific Rim countries (inclusive of Canada), and in late October 2015 reached an agreement for the Trans-Pacific Partnership (TPP). The agreement was signed early in 2016, the final year of Obama's eight-year administration, and included measures to lower non-tariff and tariff barriers and create dispute settlement procedures. The economic value of the partnership has been debated extensively, but its larger value was geopolitical. It provided a point of unity for most of the countries of the western Pacific, along with the United States, Canada, Australia, and New Zealand.

China was not part of the partnership, and in its comments regarded the partnership as economic and political containment similar to that used in Europe against the Soviet Union in the aftermath of the Second World War. The Chinese president at the time, Hu Jintao, stated that the United States had *strengthened its military deployments in the Asia-Pacific region, strengthened the US-Japan military alliance, strengthened strategic cooperation with India, improved relations with Vietnam, inveigled Pakistan, established a pro-American government in Afghanistan, increased arms sales to Taiwan, and so on. They have extended outposts and placed pressure points on us from the east, south, and west.* [Cited in Robert Kagan's 2012 book, *The World America Made*.]

The 2016 election of President Donald Trump brought most of these earlier initiatives to an end. As one of his first acts in late January 2017, President Trump withdrew the United States from the partnership, despite its ratification by the other eleven signatory countries.

Since then, American policy in the region has largely consisted of efforts to denuclearize North Korea and create a trading and economic relationship with China that is more favourable to the United States. Needless to say, those efforts, characterized by large statements and little achievement, have put American allies in the region on edge and created large concerns about the United States as a guarantor of security. In the interval, the original eleven countries of the TPP have come together in a revised TPP called the Comprehensive and Progressive Agreement for Trans-Pacific Partnership.

Central to any understanding of security relationships in Asia and beyond has been the exponential growth of China's economy. In the aftermath of the death of Mao in 1976, the adoption and encouragement of policies promoting market forces, along with Nixon's decision "to go to China" in 1974, completely changed the policies of all countries in dealing with China. Even the harsh reaction to a burgeoning effort for greater political freedom in 1989, which illustrated the duality of Chinese policy, did not provide any long-term second-guessing or examination of policies with regard to China. Today, the conflicting views between Beijing and Hong Kong, similarly, will not provide the basis for any concerted action or long-lasting effort to alter Beijing's "one China" policies. The idea of "two systems" is now a historical footnote and is as important as the views of the United Kingdom on the issue.

Chinese economic growth throughout this period fueled economic growth at home, and in the view of many, significantly fueled economic growth globally. The policies of other countries, including the United States, gave encouragement and support. All countries, and especially their business communities, in one way or another, created large offshore arrangements in China. While there are efforts in play for the cancellation of these arrangements and the "re-shoring" of supply lines, these would entail large economic costs and would seriously undermine the promised and needed economic rebounding in the aftermath of COVID-19.

The China "blame game" on the coronavirus and America's self-created economic difficulties may provide some comfort for the November elections, but it will do little to alter the fundamental involvement of China in the global economy. As well, given Trump's record in dealing with China, there is no confidence that serious or long-lasting policies will emerge from the madhouse that is the White House. President Trump will need all the help he can get for the November 2020 election, and another meaningless trade "agreement" with President Xi Jinping in the coming weeks will dampen any suggestion the United States is serious about dealing with the issues involved.

In a month or so from the time of writing, the United States will decide whether President Donald Trump is re-elected or if Joe Biden will become the forty-sixth president of the United States. Much will be said about China in these coming months, but there is no possibility that what will be said will have any serious effect on Chinese policies. It must be assumed that China will concentrate on the restoration of economic growth rates comparable to its pre-COVID-19 days. In doing so, its value as a destination for a large volume of the world's natural resources, its value as a source for many of the products the world is interested in purchasing, and its ability to take and manage large geopolitical-based economic initiatives will continue.

In political matters, there is no reason to expect there will be significant change in the recent actions by China. The Sinification initiatives in its western regions, including in Tibet and Xinjiang, will continue; the "two systems" concept that characterized Hong Kong's relationship with Beijing will be amended at will; transportation initiatives under the Belt and Road program for improved connections to the rest of the world will not lessen; China's marine boundaries in the East and South China Seas will become more pronounced, and the "facts on the water" will be accepted grudgingly by the directly affected countries—and in turn, India will continue to live with an unsettled border with China, where occasional clashes will always be possible.

In this atmosphere, there will not be significant enthusiasm for collective countering actions and activities by other countries. An early indication of this is the response of the countries of the European Union. Their economies are fragile and under some measure of stress from the departure of the United Kingdom from the EU, the effects of the COVID-19 pandemic, and the implementation of centralized debt management policies. All of the countries in the

EU see the economic relationship with China as an essential element in the restoration of their economic well-being, and there will be little to no interest in supporting policies aimed at China to force change in its actions and activities.

The policies of Japan, South Korea, Vietnam, and Taiwan will be the most affected by this changed political and economic environment. For each, it will be their understanding of American policy that will influence them politically. So far, all have been shaken by the shambolic actions of United States under President Trump, which they first hear about in his 2 a.m. tweets. In that sense, all four countries will wait to see the results from the November 2020 election as a starting point for their individual reassessments of their relationships with China. The re-election of President Trump will see all four countries contemplating changes in their China policies. Most likely, all four will see the accommodation of an outwardly aggressive China as being a large element in their policies in the coming years. Even if Biden is elected, the four countries will not be confident in reliable American support as China aggressively asserts its role in the region.

12. Comings and Goings in Global Power Relationships

> *"But there are also unknown unknowns—the ones we don't know we don't know. And if one looks throughout the history of our country and other free countries, it is the latter category that tend to be the difficult ones."* — Donald Rumsfeld, 2002

As indicated earlier, assessing the future during a period of large global changes is not for the timid. However, as others have realized during earlier times, there is a need for tentative ideas on how to keep moving ahead into the unknown. When the invasion of Afghanistan was still underway and Iraq was in the works, the American secretary of defence in 2002 ruefully and uncharacteristically spoke: "But there are also unknown unknowns—the ones we don't know we don't know. And if one looks throughout the history of our country and other free countries, it is the latter category that tend to be the difficult ones." Donald Rumsfeld's comments still surprise as he was one of the authors of so much that is wrong in American foreign policy today.

Russia. The global power and influence of the Soviet Union has disappeared, and as an old Russian joke would have it, "Russia has long been a country with an unpredictable past." Restoration efforts by the current president, Vladimir Putin, to give Russia some semblance of that power and influence, while significant, are not likely to succeed—but this does reflect its "unpredictable past." Putin's confusion of his personal agenda with the hopes of many Russians is temporal. His efforts to recreate a global role for Russia, largely based on ideas common to the Romanovs, carry their own contradictions and illusions. There is little consent, and with large internal divisions and an unwillingness by many Russians to accept sleight of hand, constitutional change does not provide a solid foundation for the future.

But Russia lingers on as we enter the twilight of future forecasting. It must be accounted for, not for the light it may provide during the years ahead, but for the ongoing influence it will seek to exercise. In some ways, Russia's exploitation of the digital world of global communications may be more influential than its earlier use of assassination, imprisonment, and torture. The United States' reaction to the overwhelming evidence of Russian promotion and support of Donald Trump as a presidential candidate demonstrates two things: the skill of the Russian system in doing so, and the inability or unwillingness of the United States to deal with what went on and still goes on. This will stand as one of the great national follies when future historians look at the early years of the twenty-first century.

Russia's future will be determined not by the artificial glorification of past events, but in the utilization of its unique attributes of place and people. The place is enormous. It is the largest country (twice the size of Canada, the second-largest country), has over 12 percent of the world's land mass, borders sixteen countries, contains eleven of the world's twenty-four time zones, and encompasses parts of Europe, Asia, and Central Asia. It is nonpareil. It is a place of immense resources. It can become one of the great positive influencers in our atmospherically poisoning world. The word "Siberia" once conjured up images of dread and darkness, but as with northern Canada, it can become a source of fundamental influence for the moderation of extreme climate change. As the world comes to accept there is only one "climate" for our benighted piece of space dust, Russia is not only important but essential to our collective survival.

Territory is not Russia's only key attribute. We have come to know the "Russians" well in the last half of the twentieth century. The threat represented by its vast pile of nuclear weapons and its associated global delivery system caused the Americans, from time to time, to bemoan their perceived "gaps" in long-range bombers and missiles. However, Norman Jewison, in his 1966 film *The Russians Are Coming, The Russians Are Coming*, lessened the tension in showing that the Russians put on their socks one foot at a time, and détente was born.

Within the shorthandedness of "Russian" as a descriptor, there is a vast melange of peoples representing great diversity of ethnicity, language, and religion. Occasionally, these peoples have broken through the crust of Russian control. At the time of the Soviet Union's implosion, we began to hear about Chechnya and its population of over one million who decided they wanted to reach independence from the Soviet Union. Three wars later, with the emergence of a local Putin satrap, Chechnya was firmly maintained as an integral part of the Russian "federation," and not an independent country. In the same period, there was unrest in Dagestan with similar efforts to cut ties with Moscow. The Dagestanis, comprising multiple nationalities, did not even warrant a war; they were beaten back into Russian conformity by Russian security forces.

Today, across the twenty-three "republics" that form part of the new Russia, there continues to be some measure of unrest and desire for independence, or at least for some lessening of Moscow's hard controls. Yet, as in the 1930s, the hammer is the only instrument used to ensure Russian control. In many of these "republics," ethnicity, language, and religion remain as a powerful impulse for greater freedom and independence. Russification has eroded this impulse in some of the "republics" in the hope that, over time, the local forces for change will disappear. It is a gamble that Moscow has been prepared to make, but in a world where people can only be controlled through force, the ideas that have given them survival over the past hundred years live on. In the end, it may be the very size and diversity of Russia's lands that keep it from ever achieving what the Soviet Union did for seventy years.

A recent example of internal tensions in Russia was the arrest in early July 2020 of the popular local governor in eastern Khabarovsk Krai. The governor defeated a Kremlin-selected candidate in the 2018 elections and enjoyed considerable local support. The governor, following his detention by security forces, was flown to Moscow where he pleaded not guilty to charges of murder supposedly committed some twenty years ago. This governor, not unlike many local leaders across Russia, had a murky past, but it surprised many that Moscow had to search back twenty years in order to find grounds for his arrest. Most likely it was his public differences with President Putin that led to his downfall. This is the latest demonstration of Moscow's control of all parts of the country, and it is not significantly different than it was during the rule of the Communist Party of the Soviet Union. Khabarovsk Krai is a small territory with just over one million people in southeast Siberia, bordering on the Sea of Japan, with the island of Sakhalin as the eastern boundary of the sea.

Russification is a first cousin of Sinification. Perhaps in a large, diverse country where leaders seek to impose commonality, Russification will succeed, in the spirit of the hopeful phrase "out of many, one." The Russia of today may be an early United States when this was *e pluribus unum,* the American national motto. This shared commonality of a fundamental national policy may also suggest the current Russian–Chinese period of cooperation could sustain longevity.

India. India is often included when the term "superpower" is used in characterizing the relative position of countries. In many ways, India's attributes compare easily with those of others. Its population is expected to exceed that of China in the next two or so decades, and India's peoples are, on average, the youngest in the world. Geographically, it overlooks the major sea routes linking Asia and Europe; it militarily dominates neighbouring countries, except for China; its economy is diverse, among the largest in the world and continues to show exceptional growth; large numbers of Indians were indentured or migrated to several countries (Fiji, Indonesia, Malaysia, Singapore, Guyana, and Trinidad and Tobago),forming significant political, economic, and distinctive cultural groupings; its cuisine is global in use and enjoyment; and above all, India has maintained a democratic system of government where its diversity gives new and unexpected meaning to the concept of "nation-state."

Its history, however, provides a continuing heavy hand on the emergence of a coherent, confident, and decisive place where the metrics of "superpower" are accentuated. India's long history, as long as that of China, with the emergence of a structured way of life along with religions, continues to provide it with a uniqueness among the countries of the world. Languages, religions, and social and geographic differentiation in India provide a rich fusion requiring judicious and sophisticated governance.

There are hundreds of languages still in use, with thirty or more with a million speakers and more than a dozen with ten million or more. Hindi dominates, with approximately 40 percent of the population (five hundred million or more), but Bengali, Marathi, Telugu, Tamil, Gujarati, and Urdu each have tens of millions of speakers. There are twenty-three constitutionally recognized official languages, with Hindi and English used by the central government in official exchanges. State governments, numbering twenty-eight, use their officially designated language. Greenberg's diversity index measures the probability that two people selected from the population at random will have different mother tongues. The index ranges from 0,with everyone having the same mother tongue, to 1, with no two people having the same mother tongue. On this scale India rates .914, or fourteenth in language diversity, while Canada rates .603, China .521, the United States .333, and Russia .283.

India's religions—Hinduism, Jainism, Buddhism, and Sikhism—contribute a second large element of diversity. Islam and Christianity, religions largely associated with invaders, provide a further complicating aspect in the daily lives of Indians and their governance. Hinduism, practiced by 80 percent of the population (over one billion people), dominates, but Islam, representing nearly 15 percent of the population, or 175 million people, provides some measure of conflict on a daily basis. It is a conflict that is exploited by Pakistan in the continuing war over Jammu and Kashmir. Largely associated with Hinduism, but not exclusively, the social and economic categorization of people into various castes continues to present large issues of governance. These problems were accentuated during the British colonial period, but since independence, New Delhi has, through a variety of positive action programs, sought to provide educational and economic opportunities for those at the lower end of the caste system, identified generally as "untouchables."

In addition to the twenty-eight states in India, there are also eight "union territories" administered from New Delhi, plus seventeen "autonomous areas" allowing for some measure of independence from state governments. The union territories include Jammu and Kashmir and Ladakh, which are central to the border disputes with Pakistan and China, respectively. The richness in language, culture, and religion represented by this geographic diversity is enormous. Various reorganizations since independence have sought to create states and territories with language cohesion, and in doing so, have reduced a source of political tension within the federation. It has occasionally provided the basis for the creation of independence movements, but these have been contained by strong actions by the central government. Today there is a degree of calmness within the Indian Federation that has not been evident since its creation in 1947.

India's diversity is seen by many as the reason why it will not achieve "superpower" status when compared to China. This is a premature judgement. India has achieved the success enumerated above based on its diversity. Its continuing and successful democratic system regularly seeks the consent of its people at all levels, is a remarkable achievement, and is perhaps the most unique in the world. Its growth over the past seventy-five years since independence has had its highs and lows, but the steadfast adherence to obtaining the regular consent of the people provides great confidence for the future. China differs in that the narrowness of its government structures and the lack or unwillingness to subject its legitimacy through universal consent mechanisms should be a large concern. History is replete with the death of such systems and there is little reason to believe that the Chinese system will be an exception. Political structures are not immutable, and narrowly based ones create their own conditions for large change and their possible disappearance.

As mentioned earlier, successful countries, and even the unsuccessful ones, carry their own seeds of collapse. India is no exception to that firm rule of history. In India, and, as will be seen below, in the United States, the success so far with a collective urge for greater success on issues associated with diversity is an essential element in assuring a better future. India, as a unity, is a recent phenomenon, as in some interpretations the concept of India was an abstraction except in a geographical sense. It was the presence of the British and the emergence of a collective local force to see the British disappear that ensured the creation, maintenance, and promotion of diversity. Seventy years later, there are now leaders who believe they can play around with the success diversity has provided and implement policies of division, disunity, and disparagement. The present prime minister, Narendra Modi, and his government of Hindu nationalism, is such a leader. If disparagement replaces diversity as a large element of national policy, then the very seeds of collapse will have been cultivated.

United States. Assessing the future of the United States in the whirlpool created by President Donald Trump is not something that is easily assayed or done with confidence. Changes as a result of the November 2020 elections can be expected, but estimating the extent of the change is similar to playing three-dimensional chess. While in chess, the pieces maintain established constants in their motions, in politics, it is the chessboard on which the players play that moves constantly.

That is the United States of today. Understanding the movement of the "chessboards" is part of our daily news cycle, and in the view of many, our daily entertainment. But that is far too cynical. Canada is not alone in trying to understand these changes; what happens in the United States, unlike the catchy phrase involving Vegas, does not stay in the United States. The United States has been and remains the largest force in the world, and its understanding must remain as the first law of our common futures.

In assaying that future, there is much on which our judgement can be based. Gibbon took six volumes to describe what happened to the Romans and he, writing a thousand or more years after their fall, had the comfort and confidence of knowing the conclusion. But we are in our proverbial Newfoundland boat not knowing if it is still being built or collapsing in the wind and waves of our vast global ocean.

An example of our great confusion in understanding the United States of today occurred on July 6, 2020. On that day, the United States Supreme Court ruled that "states can require members of the Electoral College to cast their votes for the presidential candidates they had pledged to support," in the reporting words of the *New York Times*. The electoral college is, in the understanding of many, a minor quirky constitutional provision that has existed since the days of George Washington, meant as the final step in the legalization of the election of an American president. But today, after more than two hundred years of electing American presidents, it took a Supreme Court decision to confirm that members of the college, *if directed by the laws of the state they represented,* had to vote in accordance with their previously made pledge.

The corollary, of course, is that should a state not direct its electoral college members to vote as they pledged, then the president could be elected on their personal whims and fancies. In theory, 435 members of the electoral college could elect the president. The college, using the language of digital communications, is of course "virtual." Even the Academy of Motion Picture Arts and Sciences has some seven thousand voting members in order to award Oscars. Some would argue that the American Supreme Court might have a greater sense of the importance of the American president and the hundreds of years of effort needed to sustain the democratic principle of "rep by pop" than is represented by its recent decision. But behind the continuing life of the electoral college mechanism is the dark hand of racism. Some states see the college as a symbol of its earlier ability to limit and control the voting power of American Blacks, and any effort to see it eliminated, no matter how far-fetched, will engage automatic opposition.

In understanding the United States, there is a sense that the "perfect union" of its creation is not as "perfect" as the artificial mythologies suggest, but one where large "truths" are no longer "sacred and un-deniable" nor "self-evident." Fundamental in that not "all men are created equal" and the one "unalienable" right of "Life, Liberty and the Pursuit of Happiness" is not available to large numbers of Americans. Importantly, the giving of "just powers" by the "consent of the governed" has been corrupted by the power of money, in which large numbers of Americans are voting suppressed, injured, or ignored by the process.

In large measure, it is because of this lack of "consent" that the streets of Minneapolis, Washington, Portland, and Baltimore now reflect the streets of Cairo, Hong Kong, and Sao Paulo. All are filled with people whose hands are raised in protest demonstrating that the "consent of the governed" has not been obtained. In the United

States, this is the five-hundred-year tragedy of slavery and the collective domination of one people by another. Despite the worldwide banning of chattel slavery, a murderous and divisive civil war, an emancipation declaration, and numerous civil rights laws and Supreme Court decisions, the depiction of one Black man being held face-down on a street in Minneapolis by the boots of four white police officers has shaken the core of the American federation. This has happened before and will happen again, illustrating the inability of the American federation to see this historical injustice removed from its midst.

The Trump presidency is not the cause of this injustice nor its only perpetuator. Rather, President Trump represents the complete capture of the American political system by corporate America. In its January 21, 2010 5–4 decision, *Citizens United v. Federal Election Commission*, the United States Supreme Court prohibited the enactment of laws restricting independent expenditures, inclusive of corporations, for political communications. While one Republican senator saw this as "an important step in the direction of restoring 'First Amendment rights,'" then President Barack Obama stated that the decision "gives the special interests and their lobbyists even more power in Washington." A dissenting associate justice of the Supreme Court wrote that the decision of the majority was "a rejection of the common sense of the American people, who have recognized a need to prevent corporations from undermining self-government."

Corporations represent enormous amounts of money and influence within the American political system. They use this power to obtain governments in Washington that are fully supportive of their needs. All successful political campaigns in the United States are based on vast amounts of corporate money. Presidential campaigns now need one billion or more dollars, while the campaigns of senators and members of congress are based on hundreds of millions. The *Citizens United* decision provided the legalization for this non-democratic but dominating aspect of American political life.

The measurement of the electorate has had a long history in American politics. The views of the voter on a full range of public issues are assumed to form another fundamental element in the American political system. The twitches and tempers of the electorate, both nationally and at the constituency level, are measured by a vast army of pollsters determined to provide candidates with information that might give them victory. This, along with the source of money, produces a political class of leaders who lead from behind, where there is little room or reason for independence or thoughtfulness.

Today, money and polling have combined with the corruption of the digital global age of communications. This provides the ability to reach into the minds of millions and provide them with information, both false and accurate, that creates big opinions. This, in turn, is now measured by polling. This system is still at an early stage but there are recent examples that establish its catastrophic consequences. The first was the use of the technique to create a narrow victor in the British referendum on continued membership in the European Union. The narrow victory of the Brexit proponents has been examined and there is sufficient evidence to support the idea that there was widespread corruption of the information used by many to vote in favour of the exit. Needless to say, even without the impact of COVID-19 on the people of Britain, the stupidity of that decision will affect not only the well-being of the British, but will influence further developments in Europe and the world.

The second example of the misuse of digital communications occurred with the election of Donald Trump in 2016. Russia's role in that misuse has been minutely detailed by the Muller report, and while its language is that of a lawyer versed in moderation, the conclusions demonstrate the large impact of Russian manipulation in the American electoral process. These manipulations included direct interference in the 2016 presidential election, conspiracy, and/or coordination between Trump's campaign and Russia, as well as the obstruction of justice. There is some evidence that China was equally involved in this process, but that subject has yet to be examined in detail.

These, then, are the enormous frailties of the American political system. These frailties also include six decades of failed foreign wars and the ultimate failure of American foreign policy in exercising its global leadership role. So far there are few signs that there are serious efforts underway to moderate these frailties, and the November 2020 elections may be the first opportunity to see if Americans are willing to do so. If there are no changes at the presidential level nor in the Senate, then the United States will offer little hope to a world in need of leadership and direction. It is this American dilemma, more than anything else, that will shape our world for the rest of the twenty-first century. And it is the breaching of the rock representing the role of China that will be the test.

China. Earlier, the modern role of China and its rise to global power and influence over the last five decades was examined. There are two unique elements that bear emphasis. The first is the relatively minor role military power has played in China's present status. The word "relative" is used advisedly as there are large signs that the tiger has sharp claws and those claws are getting bigger and sharper as China moves from a role of influence to one of domination in East Asia and beyond. The use of its military has been relatively minor in the four wars in which its armed forces have been committed. On the Korean Peninsula in 1950, the size of its military intervention put paid to any expectation the forces representing the UN would get to the Yula River or prevail beyond a draw. But on the Indian, Soviet, and Vietnamese borders, the use of military power, while dominating, was comparatively restrained.

The PLA experience in 1950 on the Korean Peninsula was with an army of peasants where advantage was gained by numbers and previous experience fighting in a hostile environment. Experiences at war with India, the Soviet Union, and Vietnam created a continuing drive to build a military force not based on numbers but on training, professional leadership, and equipment modernization. Today, the Chinese military is the largest military force in the world, with a budget second only to that of the United States. It is self-sufficient in much of its modern military equipment and must be considered the region's most sophisticated in power projection. However, its ability to project military power beyond East Asia has never been tested and it is unlikely that it will be in the next decade or so. However, the PLA is not staying at home, as it is now a participant in UN military missions in other countries.

In an effort to produce comparative military strength indicators, a Credit Suisse report in 2015 gave the United States a score (based on 100) of 94, while Russia and China were scored at 80 and 79. Japan received a score of 72; India, 69; South Korea, 52; Pakistan, 41;

Taiwan, 32; and Australia, 30. For comparative familiarity, Canada was scored at 10. In expenditure terms, the annual defence budget in 2018 for the United States was $648.8 billion, China was $250 billion, India was $66.5 billion, Russia was $61.4 billion, South Korea was $43.1 billion, and Canada was $21.8 billion. Taiwan spent $10.4 billion in the same year. The United States and China collectively spent approximately one half of the world's total defence budget on their militaries.

Such numbers have value but are not in any way conclusive. These numbers do conclusively show that China, central to the East Asia region, is clearly the dominant military power, as the United States and Russia both have larger responsibilities, both nationally and globally. Account must also be made of the nuclear weapons and associated delivery systems that are available to the potentially contending parties. Six of the world's nine nuclear powers are involved and all have nuclear weapons that shape their geopolitical and regional strategies. The United States, Russia, and China are all signatories to the 1970 Non-Proliferation Treaty, while India and Pakistan have acknowledged deliverable nuclear weapons and have declared "no first use" policies. North Korea acceded to the treaty in 1985 but withdrew in 2003 following its first detonation of a nuclear device.

There is no sense that the views of Mao Zedong on the use of nuclear weapons are shared by the leaders of China today. Equally, there is no sense that the views of some Americans during both the Korean and Vietnam wars—that the use of nuclear weapons should have been considered—are in play. Nevertheless, the availability of nuclear weapons to potentially contending parties must be a factor in any discussion of developments in East Asia in the coming years. China has stayed out of current United States–Russia disputes concerning their bilateral treaties on nuclear weapons and their associated delivery systems, and it can be assumed that its policies on the use of nuclear weapons conforms to the NPT. But there is one truth from the historical lessons of all war: the ending of a war is never foretold by its beginning.

The second unique element in the rise of China as a global power is its skillful use of its own economic development in co-opting worldwide support. Since the death of Mao Zedong in 1976, China

China in a Changing World

has transformed from a self-indulgent, cannibalistic society to one with the world's most dynamic economic system supporting enormous growth at home and around the world. It is not an exaggeration to suggest that the world's economy rests on China's shoulders. In large measure, one man was the source of this transformation.

Deng Xiaoping was still in purgatory upon the death of Mao, but his inordinate skills and experience carried him to the top of the Party, and within two years he was its paramount chief, although not actually occupying the top positions. His economic reforms, characterized by some as "socialism with Chinese characteristics," had more to do with China than with socialism, and he remains revered today as the architect of Modern China. More than anything, his reforms carried hundreds of millions of Chinese out of poverty and into a middle class of well-educated and experienced citizens. This transformation moved China into the world's economy, and it became the major supplier of goods, services, and investment to all countries. In turn, China purchased large amounts of the world's resources and products.

These were not unilateral changes. China's own growth was based on a society starved for the benefit of its own revolution and completely open to the massive social changes that twentieth-century industrialization involved. Its growth from village to city preoccupied hundreds of millions of people and the result was the creation of an urban proletariat. The world beyond China was equally changing from one where industry needed the large wrench and hammer to one needing the nimbleness of mind and fingers and enhancement of sight. Production-sharing arrangements within and between countries, the demand for small value labour differences, the devaluation of unionization, and the development of efficient worldwide transportation and communications systems provided China with the opportunity to engage the world as a valued economic partner. The world was not inattentive.

A China striving for its place in the world, accompanied by the efficient production of goods and services at a cost less than would normally be available in the West, ensured its warm welcome into that world. "Made in China" transformed from a label indicative of questionable quality and late-night humour to one that is today a sign of quality and preference. Global industries were the first to see the value offered by China, and in less than a decade, long-established European and American industries were transferring production to places in China. In doing so, they maintained consumer prices at levels that maintained consumption. Cars, electronics, consumer goods, and food soon acquired "Made in China" labels.

Surprisingly, these changes to the location of production did not seriously undermine the economic well-being of the countries utilizing China as a major source for goods and services. There were often localized disruptions and dislocations when a factory closed or moved to another location in-country or out of country. But economic growth in the countries most affected did not diminish appreciably; rather, there was positive growth, and in some, labour participation in the economy reached near levels of full employment.

Not surprisingly, then, governments throughout the world were less concerned with limiting the economic role of China, and instead provided support. Many governments sought trade agreements to manage the relationship, with the expectation that any negative effects on overall trade would be controlled. In recent years, numerous bilateral agreements were signed, discussed, and proposed. It was in this context that some countries, including the United States and Canada, saw large negative imbalances on merchandising trade as something that needed correcting. But this involved possibly reducing imports from China, then developing strategies and opportunities to increase exports to China.

Even the tragedy of Tiananmen Square in the first half of 1989 did little to interrupt the growing economic importance of China to the world. Deng, in the aftermath, began to reduce his role, but in his travels, he continued to present an open and engaging face to the world, convincing many that economic reforms would lead to political reforms. During this period, the destruction of the Soviet Union convinced others that a gradually reforming China, both economically and politically, represented a great value to the world. By the time Deng died in 1997, serious discussions were underway for the inclusion of China into the World Trade Organization, newly created in 1995 as the successor to the General Agreement on Tariffs and Trade. The dismantling of some state-owned corporations and the introduction of policies that created a market economy provided an environment not significantly different from other members of the WTO. It was the success of these changes that produced an economy creating double-digit numbers of decades-long economic growth, ensuring the integration of China into the economy of the world. The 2008 self-created economic disaster in the United States even added creditability to the value of China to the economies of other countries.

In the midst of all of this, current efforts by the United States to curtail or terminate the work of the WTO is an effort to deny China the legitimacy that it gained when it became a member twenty years ago. Fortunately, the rest of the world needs the WTO, and hopefully the transitory efforts of the United States to curtail its operations will not last beyond the November 2020 elections. This is not to suggest that the WTO does not need reform and modernization. It does, but there is little appetite for either reform or modernization if China is the target. Again, many parts of the world need what China has on offer. The creation of the Chinese-dominated Asian Infrastructure Investment Bank and the Silk Road Fund provides opportunities that are already being exploited by China and other countries. This at a time when the United States practises the crude art of destruction instead of offering leadership on a range of economic issues that might be of some value to the world.

China's economic success over the past three decades cannot be gainsaid. The 2018 International Monetary Fund (IMF) list of the twenty largest economies in the world illustrates the field. Two years ago, the United States held 23.6 percent of the world's economy, while China held 15.5 percent; the next three nations (Japan, Germany, and India) held 13.3 percent combined. The next five largest (the United Kingdom, France, Italy, Brazil, and Canada) represented 12.8 percent, and the next ten (Russia, South Korea, Spain, Australia, Mexico, Indonesia, the Netherlands, Saudi Arabia, Turkey, and Switzerland) represented 13.3 percent of the world's economy. The other 173 countries of the United Nations held 21.3 percent. In specific terms, China is the largest destination for the exports of thirty-three countries and is the largest source of imports for some sixty-five countries. A decade ago, China overtook Japan as the world's second-largest economy.

There are a variety of forecasts concerning the position of China in the world's economy. Most are now useless as a result of the COVID-19 pandemic. But in one important respect, the relative success (or unsuccess) of the United States and China in dealing with the pandemic suggests that China will perform better in the years ahead than the United States. In 1980, one forecaster suggested that China would overtake the United States as the largest global economy by 2030, and when using purchasing power parity (the comparative measurement of prices) it was noted that China had surpassed the United States some six years prior. In addition, China has become the second-largest source of both outbound and inbound direct foreign investment according to one report.

This enormous economic success over some thirty years, accentuated in the last ten, has created concern among some countries and especially within the United States. Some countries, and again, especially the United States, began to look for ways to limit China's success, or to blame the success of China for their own economic problems. Unsurprisingly, increasing this concern has been the eroding of the earlier assumption that economic success in China would evolve in reforms in its political system. This has not happened. Also, with China's more robust efforts to dominate its neighbouring seas, and to some extent, to increase pressure on neighbouring countries around trade and economic matters, there is a sense that East Asia is losing some of its relative stability on security matters.

Above all, there is a growing sense that China is now challenging the United States' role in providing a guarantee of stability for Taiwan, South Korea, Japan, and beyond within Asia. It can be said with some confidence that this new state of affairs has as much to do with the ambiguity and confusion of American policy as it has to do with China's own policies. Nature abhors vacuums, irrespective of whether they are natural or geopolitical. In all of this, the American political system is operating largely on a spectrum dominated by the short term. China, on the other hand, historically and today, operates on a spectrum where the long term is the norm. A favourite tactic, demonstrated time and time again, is to let time assist in achieving large goals.

China in a Changing World

Efforts by the United States to achieve some measure of reform in its economic relationship with China is but one current example of this perspective at work. President Trump, in his loudness over Chinese trade, is not in the least bit interested in substantive changes to their economic relationship. Rather, he wishes to add a small prize to his disappearing trophy case that might demonstrate some measure of accomplishment to an increasingly suspicious electorate in time for the November 3, 2020 election. Equally, the childish blaming of China for America's pathetically ineffective response to the COVID-19 pandemic increasingly demonstrates a leader with nihilism larger and certainly more important than that of King Lear.

In the disappearance of the Roman Empire, the world largely used the stupidity of the rulers in Rome as its main ally. The destruction of Europe's empires saw the utilization of the twin forces of economic disaster at home as a result of war, and their inability to dominate faraway countries already alive to the promises of liberty and freedom in exchange for the use of their territory in war. Some countries (Malaya, Indonesia, the Philippines, Algeria, and Kenya) had to use force to relax the grasp of European powers, while others such as India and Pakistan used the force of non-violence. Yet, for most it was a "sign of the times" that saw Africa, Asia, and the Caribbean fully liberated. The Soviet Union's continental empire disintegrated with the force of weakening systems of political and economic control largely created by time's first cousin, age.

Today, the issue is the emergence of a new hegemonic empire. Unique, and unlike any in the past, China's hegemonic empire has used little to no overt force to re-establish its role in the world. Rather, the other great force in the development of our world, economic power, has dominated. China has used its size, coherence of people, and unity of purpose to reach into the world, providing and obtaining support for what it had to offer in material goods, investment, and people. Surprisingly, it offered little by way of ideology in sustaining its efforts. Instead, it was its successful emergence from a recent period of internal troubles and domination by others that was on offer in a world encountering similar problems on its own road to the future.

At this time, with COVID-19 pandemic preoccupations, there is little collective international energy available to give serious thought to what has happened in East Asia and whether or not there is a serious problem that might need concerted and collective international attention. This is a discussion awaiting the conclusions of the American 2020 elections, and importantly, a worldwide sense that COVID-19 has been returned to the netherworld. The former is a matter of a few months, while the latter will be many months, if not years in arriving. In the meantime, some consideration can be given to the issues and the associated concerns.

A Re-Elected Trump. At the time of writing in August 2020, President Trump is testing the value of blaming China for the disappearing support from his fellow citizens. On both the sickness of the economy and the illness affecting millions of Americans, the president has given a full-throat condemnation of China as the cause. A few months ago, the president was expressing his "love" for President Xi, his outstanding work underway on a new trade treaty, and the laudable efforts of China in containing the Wuhan-sourced coronavirus. Now it is the "China virus," and President Trump is insisting the large associated economic disaster in America can only be improved by significant changes in the trade policies of China. This conversion, though not as fast as that of Paul on the road to Damascus, will have little effect on the major issues involved.

But President Trump's "conversion" suggests the residual effect will live on. In a scenario where President Trump is re-elected, this could have large implications for the rest of the world. This is the political and geopolitical dimensions of future American policy. Will a re-elected Trump give rise to greater use of the phrase "we have seen nothing yet," meaning more and more extreme expressions of American policy not only in Asia but in the rest of the world? The nature of Trump's statements and actions over the past four years does suggest that an electoral victory in November 2020 will produce greater extremes in his feverish late-night explosions on social media. His "barking in the night" will have to be contained, if not accommodated.

The initial task is to provide for a rational response from both allies and enemies so that American influence is not entirely discounted.

This can be done, as was demonstrated during the first four years of President Trump's administration. But in the initial months of a re-elected Trump administration, when the effects of the global pandemic are still galloping throughout many parts of the world, the opportunity for serious miscalculation and misadventure is large. The internal system of safety within American political structures will hopefully dampen Trump's ravings and provide controls to limit the potential effects of the president's irrational inclinations towards the rest of the world.

Equally troublesome is the continued supply of re-enforcers who fill the White House and surround the president. As is evident from the experience of many countries, there is a steady supply of Goebbels, Gorings, and Ribbentrops when there are positions available near power, and Washington is no exception. Without suggesting any direct comparison with the people who surrounded and died with Hitler, the people who re-enforce a base and ignorant American president offer an ignoble spectacle and provide a dark hole where even good ideas die.

The American Congress, weakened as it is by an ever-assertive and dominating Executive, will be called upon to provide the first line of defence against a raging president. Its effectiveness in doing so, as demonstrated by its recent performance, does not give rise to any degree of confidence. The Supreme Court is even more problematic, as it seeks to accommodate its recent members and produce reasoned decisions finding general acceptance. The likely death of its oldest member, Ruth Bader Ginsburg, in the near future, will intensify the national divisions on the role of the Supreme Court.

The performance of various administrative departments and government agencies under Trump does not elicit confidence they will provide any measure of control on a re-elected President Trump. The Attorney General and the Department of Justice have largely disappeared as places of personal integrity and legal probity in the administration of justice. Many actions by the Attorney General are now based on the personal views of the president. Other parts of the government have equally succumbed to the needs of narrow economic interests. Many of the high appointments made by the president to their associated offices would even make President

Putin blush, or perhaps, seek to emulate them. The elimination of the Centers for Disease Control and Prevention from the national effort to moderate and eliminate COVID-19 from the United States will stand as one of the great human-made disasters inflicted on the American people.

These disasters, both actual and potential, pale in comparison when considered alongside the role of the American Armed Forces in a time of global uncertainty and idiosyncratic behaviour on the part of its commander-in-chief. There are some indications the present secretary of defence and the chairman of the joint chiefs of staff are increasingly sensitive to the traditional role of the military in American domestic and foreign policy. As such, they have been prepared to dampen initiatives by the president that would be contrary to that traditional role or inimical, in their view, to the long-term interests of the United States. Again, this is not without serious danger as both the secretary and the chairman could be replaced overnight with more pliable individuals by a re-elected president.

A Defeated Trump. The election of Joe Biden in November 2020 would dramatically alter the role of the United States in world affairs. It would not alter the fundamentals of the erosion of American influence as discussed above. However, the environment in which these fundamentals would be debated and solutions sought would be completely different than that which existed over the past four years. The addition of Kamala Harris as vice president suggests openness for change. Ms. Harris, an experienced, successful person in her own right and a young woman of colour with Indian, African, and Caribbean ancestry, offers a dimension in American policy creation that has not been evident for some time.

Changes in the balance of power in the Senate and maintenance of existing Democratic control of the House of Representatives would be associated with large benefits. These might be the basis on which the United States deals with its domestic problems and seeks to restore its leadership role throughout the world.

The early elements in that restoration would be a recertification of the United States' security role in Europe and in Asia. In Europe, this would be a relatively easy task, as it would increasingly be in support of the European Union as it emerges from the departure of the United Kingdom. In turn, it would involve the re-establishment of unity on the continent as it copes with COVID-19, the large debts of some members, immigrants from surrounding lands, and the threat represented by President Putin. A heavy agenda, but not one that is beyond the capabilities of the EU's leadership and resources.

China will present the largest foreign policy challenge for a newly elected President Biden. But the initial step could occur early in the life of the new Biden Administration with an announcement of a new partnership in Asia. It would also include a recertification of America's historic guarantee of security for the countries of the region beyond China. This would be relatively easy; it will be the details that will present the difficulties.

The details would centre around two large themes. First, the new administration would declare that American security interest in Asia was equal to that of its interest in Europe and there would be appropriate changes in the deployment profiles of all its military elements. Associated with such a declaration would be a clear restatement of specific American commitments for the security of Japan, South Korea, and Taiwan, and to all other countries wanting to enter into appropriate bilateral security arrangements.

The second theme would centre on China. The newly elected president would declare that the United States wanted to develop and construct a new political, economic, and security relationship with China based on cooperation, and not confrontation. The new president would declare that the United States wanted to change the bilateral relationship from one based on confrontation and competition to one that exploited the strengths of both countries. In doing so, the United States wanted a new age of cooperation to extend not only to the rest of Asia, but to the world itself, where the strengths, if not the interests, of both countries could be exploited. At the suggestion of Canadian colleagues, this could be called "realistic engagement."

Such a declaration on Asia by Biden, and an American commitment to the world, could form the basis for wide-ranging efforts to restructure both the world's political and economic relationships. The world itself has been drifting without leadership, and it would be a major achievement if the United States, in emerging from its own troubles, clearly attached its future to that of the world at large. It is this creation of hope that could alter recent American drift and the emergence of China's efforts to dominate a world that is not interested in being dominated. Equally, it could provide a direct counter to Russian efforts to re-emerge as a force in the world based on little more than the personal ambition of President Putin, historical mythologies, and kleptocracy.

The alternatives to such an approach have little to no expectation of success. Containment, to use an idea from three-quarters of a century ago, has no basis in today's reality. China is alive and well, and its vitality is now part of the well-being of billions. But involvement with China carries an element of domination that has become apparent to some of its neighbouring countries. The world is not interested in the hard line of President Xi as the only mechanism of dispute resolution, and most global leaders are open to seeing it replaced by the willingness to cooperate. To borrow a metaphor from the past, a world based on cooperation will put more chickens in more pots than all of the egotistical boasting of semi-maniacal leaders will.

Equally, the idea that the world can or will be "tough on China" is without merit or substance. This idea assumes a level of global cooperation from many that benefit from the existing policies and actions of China. The first rule of politics is not to create self-harm. A "tough on China" approach would do more harm to those who would engage it as a policy than cause significant change in Chinese policies.

Importantly, declarations by Biden—following his election or even as part of his campaign—to recommit the United States to its worldwide traditional role of leadership would provide a large positive element for the people of the United States. There is little disagreement that the past four years of Trump's administration have not been ones where the best of an America "as a city upon a hill" has been reflected. Nevertheless, the eyes of the world (if not its feet) remain fixated on the United States, and there is a large measure of goodwill towards seeing it again play a large role in the management of our only home. A return to a role that conformed less with the ideas and personal characteristics of a narrow, parochial, immoral slum landlord from New York and more with those of a Kennedy, an Obama, an Eisenhower, or a Bush would be welcomed by millions.

13. Canada and China – Problems but No Solutions

In the midst of the Chinese Cultural Revolution, Canada began negotiations for the formal recognition of the bloodiest government on the planet, and before long, there was a Canadian embassy in Beijing.

China's political and economic value to Canada has been a secondary element in its involvement in and approach to the world. It is a distant second after the United States. But at the same time, there has been a nagging sense of China's global importance that has required Canada's attention and involvement. Historically, the Pacific region did not attract the attention or interest of Canadians in comparison with the Atlantic region and the United States. Even the impact of the early migration of people from China was minor in comparison to the impact of those from Europe, and political attention emphasized control rather than encouragement. The Second World War in the Pacific, and in part, the consequential success of the Chinese Communist Revolution, changed everything. China was an ally during the Second World War in countering Japanese expansion, and Norman Bethune gave a controversial Canadian face to the revolution. In the years since, China has become the dominant actor of worldwide change and today, all countries, including Canada, give it appropriate recognition and consider if more scrutiny is necessary.

During the Second World War, Canada maintained an embassy in the Sichuanese city of Chongqing, the capital for the Nationalist forces, and assigned its first ambassador there in 1942. After the war, the capital moved to Nanjing, on the Yangtze River. Following the 1949 communist victory, Canada faced the issue of the continuation of diplomatic relations with the new government, then in Beijing. It decided to recognize the new government and was making arrangements for the exchange of ambassadors when the war in Korea began on June 25, 1950. Canada contributed troops to the UN effort and declared China guilty of aggression on the Korean Peninsula. Beijing requested the departure of the Canadian chargé and the closure of the embassy in Nanjing. In the process, Canada established and maintained diplomatic relations with the Nationalist government in Taipei but did not open an embassy there.

It was three years before the war in Korea ended with a stalemate, the division of the peninsula along the thirty-eighth parallel, and the creation of two distinct countries. During this period and for the rest of the decade, China's new revolutionary government sought to create a communal-based economy, including the collectivization of agriculture. Five-year plans of "great leaps" for large parts of the economy simply produced human misery, hunger, and the death of millions. The need to import grains provided Canada with its first significant interaction with the new regime. In the late 1950s, John Diefenbaker's government made arrangements for shipments of wheat. Agricultural products have remained as a significant element in the China–Canada trade relationship ever since.

Political and economic turmoil continued when in 1966 Mao Zedong launched the Great Proletarian Cultural Revolution. The Cultural Revolution continued for a decade, and millions more died as Mao sought to purge the country of traditional elements of society and impose his own simplistic thoughts as China's only road to the future. This revolution was in large part centred on the leadership of the Communist Party, and there were daily reports of countrywide violence as Mao and his allies executed, purged, publicly humiliated, and exiled all who were perceived as being in opposition to their rule.

The world looked on in horror, but in its midst, Canada began negotiations for the formal recognition of the bloodiest government on the planet. This was completed in 1970, and before long, there was a Canadian embassy in Beijing and Canada's relationship with Taiwan was reduced. The Americans did much the same less than two years later, and they even contributed the ultimate sign of approval with a week-long presidential visit. Even the protests of early 1989 ending in the Tiananmen Square massacre, or more recent protests in Hong Kong on its status within China, did not occasion a significant or long-lasting adverse reaction by Canada or other countries.

For the last fifty years, Canadian foreign policy gave ongoing and positive recognition to China. There were frequent prime ministerial and ministerial visits, the Team Canada group wandered the Middle Kingdom looking for specific economic deals, and treaties were signed. There were occasional expressions of concern for certain activities by Beijing, but the relationship moved forward to the point where even extradition and free trade agreements were part of the agenda.

This hubristic world came to an end on December 1, 2018. Meng Wanzhou, the deputy chair and chief financial officer of Huawei Technologies, and daughter of its founder, Ren Zhengfei, was detained by Canadian authorities at Vancouver International Airport while she was in transit on her way to Mexico and Argentina. She was detained on an extradition warrant issued at the request of the United States. The American request was based on allegations of bank fraud in connection with Huawei's control of a company believed to have violated American economic sanctions involving Iran. Huawei Technologies Co. was founded in 1987 and since has become one of the world's largest telecommunications companies, outdistancing Ericsson and Samsung, and is close to doing the same with Apple. Huawei has pride of place in China's economic transformation and role in the world. To negatively affect it is to touch the heart of the new China.

China reacted immediately. In less than ten days, two Canadians became guests of the Chinese prison system. On December 10, 2018, Michael Kovrig, an employee of the Canadian Foreign Service, on leave of absence with the International Crisis Group in Beijing, was detained. On the same day, Michael Spavor, a consultant active in North Korean business and investment matters, was also in jail. The lives and careers of both were tied to the affairs of East Asia; they have both lived for periods in China and Korea. Kovrig speaks Mandarin while Spavor speaks Korean. Both are still in prison, which in China is harsh and tightly controlled, with limited or no contact with family or officials of the Canadian government. This is in stark contrast with the at-home detention of Meng in Vancouver. Chinese authorities have alleged that both Kovrig and Spavor violated China's national security laws. They have no substantive legal representation and the amorphous nature of Chinese legal procedures offers no assurance that these alleged violations will be or could be tested anytime soon.

Eighteen months later, the Canadian government remains frustrated by this deep and unbridgeable gap in its relationship with China. Importantly, it is struggling in how it can negotiate the release of its two citizens. The prime minister and other ministers regularly emphasize the singular importance of the matter but little specificity has emerged.

The government's response so far consists of four elements. First, the government consistently argues that the detention of Meng is in accordance with the provisions of Canadian law as it applies to extradition, and the decision of whether extradition will be granted is one for the Canadian courts. Second, the detentions of Kovrig and Spavor are arbitrary and retaliatory for the detention of Meng, and as such, the two men are hostage to her release through decisions beyond the control of the Government of Canada. Third, Canada has sought the assistance of the United States and other countries in making representations to the government of China for the release of Kovrig and Spavor. Fourth, the government says as little as possible in public relating to the actions of Beijing on other issues.

Two of these elements are standard responses in these situations. They have very little to do with the possibility they will contribute to or lead to the early release of Kovrig and Spavor. The idea that other governments will come to the assistance of the two Canadians is patently whistling in the dark of a Canadian winter's night. Most countries have their own problems with Beijing and no one is going to expend significant effort in assisting Canada. As for public statements on the matter or other issues of concern to China, these are meant to give the government some semblance of respectability as it avoids dealing with the central element of the detention dispute.

China in a Changing World

The central element of the Canadian government's response has been emphasis on the application of the principle of the "rule of law." In government statements at all levels, it is the application of this principle that will decide Meng's fate to the exclusion of all others. There is some minor value in this, as it places the government on a seemingly high plane involving a principle of democratic governments everywhere, *but it is misleading*. Canadian extradition law is the one element of the Canadian justice system where political decisions are significantly, and almost overridingly so, part of the extradition process. This is contrary to all other aspects of the Canadian justice system, where independence from politically based decision-making is totally rejected. A judicial decision to extradite or not extradite is subject to review and confirmation by the minister of justice, a politician; or the minister can refuse to initiate the associated processes for extradition; or can cancel the process at any time.

The reasons for involvement by the minister of justice are specified in the Extradition Act and provide large scope for independent action by the minister. The minister can confirm a judicial decision to extradite, deny a judicial decision to extradite, or impose a different decision. One mandatory element in ministerial review includes consideration of whether an extradition would be unjust or oppressive in all the circumstances, or whether it was made on a discriminatory basis. While a ministerial decision can be appealed to the provincial Supreme Court involved, a decision by such a court would also be subject to ministerial review and confirmation. Before the process is complete, if a person has been ordered extradited, then the individual may seek leave to appeal either a decision by the provincial Supreme Court or the minister to the Supreme Court of Canada. A decision by the Supreme Court of Canada would in turn be subject to review by the minister of justice.

A relevant extradition case of a decade or so ago involved Abdullah Khadr, the older brother of Omar Khadr, a Canadian then imprisoned at the American prison in Guantanamo Bay. While lawyers were working to have Omar released, Abdullah had returned to Canada, and in late 2005, was arrested on the basis of an American extradition request and was denied bail. Four and a half years later, in August 2010, an Ontario Superior Court Justice denied the American extradition request and Abdullah Khadr was released.

The Attorney General of Canada (also the minister of justice) appealed the Superior Court's decision on behalf of the United States to the Ontario Court of Appeal. Less than a year later, on May 6, 2011, three members of the Court of Appeal affirmed the lower court's decision and voted unanimously to deny the request of the United States for Abdullah Khadr's extradition. The federal minister of justice sought to appeal the decision to the Supreme Court of Canada but on November 3, 2011, the court announced that it would not review the earlier decisions, and in doing so ended the American request for Khadr's extradition. The minister of justice decided not to exercise his authority under the Extradition Act. In comments made to the media in the aftermath of the decision by the Ontario Court of Appeals, Dennis Edney, one of Abdullah Khadr's lawyers, stated, "When a U.S. government or any foreign government steps into a Canadian court they have to arrive with clean hands."

Edney, in his comments on the American request for the extradition of Abdullah Khadr, succinctly stated a key element in all extradition cases, and the reason why there is a political dimension included in the decision-making surrounding such cases. As the Abdullah Khadr case illustrates, the need for "clean hands" on the part of requesting governments is essential. There is no guarantee that this will be the case in all requests for extradition. But it is rare for Canadian courts involved in extradition cases to do much more than identify the individual involved, and ensure that dual criminality is evident and a prima facie case involving the crime is presented.

In Abdullah Khadr's case, the extradition judge identified two categories of cases dealing with the need for "clean hands" on the part of requesting states. The first category implicates the fairness of the hearing while the second category, or residual category, is "unrelated to the fairness of the hearing but involving state conduct which undermines the integrity of the judicial process." The judge concluded that the Khadr case fell within the residual category, as one of those exceptional cases that involves state misconduct that contravenes fundamental notions of justice, and which undermines the justice system. "The extrajudicial misconduct in this case does not, in the narrow procedural sense, compromise the fairness of this extradition hearing. However, that is not to say the conduct of the Requesting State is not linked or connected to this proceeding. I disagree with the submission by counsel for the Attorney General that there is no nexus between the abuse and the fairness of this hearing. On the contrary, in a broader sense the gross misconduct that occurred in Pakistan very much affects these proceedings in Canada. The basis of this case has its genesis in the serious misconduct by the Requesting State. The Requesting State is seeking a benefit from this court, committal, based on evidence derived from its own misconduct."

In another illustrative and recent case, a Canadian, Hassan Diab, was extradited to France in connection with the bombing of a synagogue in Paris in 1980. He was imprisoned for over three years in France. The French judicial system could not find conclusive evidence supportive of Diab's involvement, and he was released and allowed to return to Canada. At the time of his extradition in June 2011, the extradition judge noted that the French government's evidence was "convoluted, very confusing, with conclusions that are suspect," and went on to note that "the prospects of conviction in the context of a fair trial seem unlikely."

Meng's judicial process has now lasted over eighteen months and has involved one court decision. The decision in May 2020 only confirmed the American request for extradition met the "dual criminality" standard in that the allegations of American crimes were crimes in Canada as well. However, that decision has little to do with the court's ultimate decision and Meng's fate. As similar cases demonstrate, the ultimate judicial decision on extradition is years away, as it would seem both the Canadian government acting on behalf of the American government and the counsel representing Meng are inclined to delay matters as much as possible. They do so to exploit the possibility of action by the American government that could be characterized by the court as "gross misconduct," which would thus undermine the legitimacy of the American request for extradition.

Lending evidence of significant further delay is the fact that the courts in Canada and elsewhere have been seriously affected by measures taken to deal with the COVID-19 pandemic. The possibility of an early decision by the court dealing with Meng's case is extremely low. In late summer 2020, it was announced that the trial was scheduled to begin in April 2021.

These events in a Canadian court have a direct and immediate impact on the lives of the two Canadians imprisoned in difficult circumstances in China. Both Kovrig and Spavor have been imprisoned for over eighteen months, and while events in Canada are generally within the purview of all Canadians, the circumstances of these two Canadians have been kept completely hidden. It must be assumed that they are hostage to developments in Canada. In addition to the harshness of their imprisonment, there is no knowledge available about the effect of COVID-19 on prisoners in China. There is no reason to believe that they are being more effectively shielded than the general population.

There is an answer to this dilemma while staying well within the soft boundaries of the "rule of law." The minister of justice could exercise his authority at any time under the Extradition Act and deny the American request for extradition. He could act immediately by cancelling the order to proceed with the legal process of extradition or exercise ministerial judgement now on the American request. The reasons for doing so would include the following:

- The American decision to request Meng's extradition was not a legitimate effort to prosecute a crime but rather a reflection of broader American policy to change its trading relationship with China and support its unilateral actions against Iran.

- The political influence on judicial matters in the United States is extraordinary at this time and there can be no expectation this will change in the coming months. The looming election and need of the current president to provide indications of success could include an agreement with China on trade matters.

- Huawei, the company directly involved in the activities of Meng, has been the target of American policy efforts under the broad premise that it represents a threat to U.S. national security. This view is not reflected in Canadian policy.

- The time necessary for the Canadian courts to reach a decision creates extraordinary danger for the lives and well-being of the two imprisoned Canadians.

Canadians are frustrated by the lack of success and there is growing public antagonism towards China's actions. There are daily commentaries on the detentions and much advice about what Canada should do. Some of this advice could be inimical to the well-being of Kovrig and Spavor, further prolonging their detentions or making their treatment by the Chinese authorities worse. The advice for suggested actions by Canada includes the following:

- Responding effectively to each of these examples of China's assaults on a rules-based international system will require significant reserves of Canadian courage and resolve.
- Canada is increasingly out of step when allies are expressing reservations about China's lack of transparency. Canada seems unable or unwilling to make the same declaration. Canadians are still locked in this tendency to speak only in praiseworthy language, and therefore only to praise what China is doing, rather than speak honestly about what is happening.
- The Canadian government needs to protest in the strongest terms and find a way to ensure that consular visits can resume, especially during the COVID-19 pandemic.
- Canada must carefully evaluate the extent to which it can engage with China economically and whether that would require compromising national security or conceding an "if you can't beat them then, join them" abandonment of Canadian support for justice, fairness, reciprocity, and human rights.
- The only minor leverage Canada has in pushing for the two Canadians' release is its own soft power, and the reputational damage done to Beijing when Ottawa raises the cases. Failing to send that message consistently tells Beijing that the cost of their actions is not just small, but temporary.
- If, as a result of the B.C. Supreme Court ruling, it could take months or years to decide the outcome of Meng's extradition case, the future of the two Michaels appears no less certain.

- The situation is now at the point where Chinese-Canadians are afraid to write to their federal MPs on matters related to China or money laundering, as Alex Lee, an activist with the Alliance Hong Kong Canada, has stated: "People are saying, will my name be handed to the Chinese Communist Party by somebody on the staff that works for my MP?"
- Yet, restraint hasn't accomplished much either, and frankly, it goes against the values Canada stands for. Canada should invoke its "Magnitsky" law under which it can legally impose sanctions on corrupt or rights-abusing foreign officials. In other words, hit China's rulers in the pocketbook.
- Canada must follow through with action if the Chinese enforce the new law. That might take the form of asset freezes and travel bans against Chinese officials. As Alex Lee further stated, "We need to come off the fence and support those who are trying to preserve the rights promised them."
- And there is much Canada can do, alone and with its allies. China's growing belligerence coupled with its role in the COVID-19 disaster has internationally tilted the balance of sentiment against it. Countries are increasingly calculating that they have less to lose by defying China than by submitting to it.

In late 2015, two Canadians, John Ridsdel and Robert Hall, were captured by the secessionist terrorist group Abu Sayyaf in the southern Philippines. Within a few months, both were executed by their captors. They died needlessly when the newly elected Liberal government refused to alter an ongoing policy and facilitate arrangements for the payment of the demanded ransoms. This policy has become an expression of a deep unfounded principle and was the result of efforts by a number of governments to counter such kidnappings as part of the global war against terrorism.

As with all such unfounded principles, when lives are on the line, it was honoured more in the breach than in its observance, as governments decided the policy had no effect on such kidnappings nor acts of terrorism generally. The newly elected Canadian government, either through inexperience in such matters or belief that the policy of not paying ransom was of some value, made inappropriate statements as the two Canadians were force-marched through the southern jungles of the Philippines. Ridsdel and Hall were executed as a result—Ridsdel in April 2016 and Hall in June. During this same period, other governments negotiated and arranged ransoms for the release of their citizens.

The fates of Ridsdel and Hall are worthy of remembrance as the government gropes for an effective policy to assist Kovrig and Spavor, imprisoned in China. Everyone with knowledge and understanding of the situation has concluded that both have been imprisoned by the government of China for bargaining in forcing the release of Meng from extradition to the United States. In plain language, they have been kidnapped, just like Ridsdel and Hall almost five years ago in the jungles of the southern Philippines.

In late June 2020, Korvig's family made an impassioned appeal to Prime Minister Justin Trudeau for action to obtain the release of Michael Kovrig and Michael Spavor. The author wrote of this development in a June article for *The Hill Times*, which stated that in responding to this appeal, the prime minister changed his position on the possible release of Meng Wanzhou in exchange for the release of Michael Kovrig and Michael Spavor. The shift occurred when he responded, during his regular morning press conference, to the public appeal by the family of Kovrig and a letter from Canadians experienced in such matters.

The prime minister declared: "The reality is releasing Meng Wanzhou to resolve a short-term problem would endanger thousands of Canadians who travel to China and around the world by letting countries know that a government can have political influence over Canada by randomly arresting Canadians." He then went back to his standard response by declaring "Canada has an independent judiciary and those processes will unfold independently of any political pressure, including by foreign governments."

The prime minister is wrong in using both of these reasons for inaction in obtaining the release of Kovrig and Spavor. His earlier exclusivity in using the "independent judiciary" or "rule of law" as supreme in extradition matters has shown to be false. The language of the Extradition Act clearly and conclusively demonstrates that the minister of justice, acting in his political capacity, is the final authority on such matters. To argue otherwise has no basis in law.

The prime minister depends on Canadians having a short memory when he uses the rule of law to buttress his views. Not so many months ago, his government attempted to interfere directly in the Canadian justice system. Even the ethics commissioner of the Parliament of Canada ruled that the prime minister improperly pressured the minister of justice of the day to fix an ongoing criminal case. In doing so, the prime minister explained this was all about saving "jobs."

Equally, the rule-of-law argument echoes with particular insincerity as thousands of Indigenous people and Canadians of colour march to demonstrate that the rule of law discriminates on the basis of historical and ongoing racism. Those arrested and those imprisoned far outnumber their relative population size in the country and the road to a better life remains highly inferior.

In shifting the basis for not acting because it would "endanger" thousands of travelling Canadians, the prime minister is as wrong as he is in using the rule-of-law argument. In a world free of COVID-19, millions of Canadians live or travel outside of Canada for reasons that have not disappeared, but are just temporarily interrupted.

The sale of Canadian passports is one of the highest in the world. Recently, the loud cries of tens of thousands of Canadians wanting to return to Canada because of the pandemic illustrates that travelling Canadians are as common as the sedentary Canadians of Little Heart's Ease or Moose Jaw. In the post-pandemic world, this travel will return. Visiting family in Chittagong, seeing the Greek islands, or studying and working abroad will continue to drive Canadians out into the world.

A singular act by the Government of Canada in successfully rescuing two Canadians will not change this. In some measure, it could well encourage more Canadians to travel, knowing their government is there to help when things go bang in the night. Foreign governments are not lurking, waiting to clap up nefarious travelling Canadians for whatever reason meets their fancy. This will not change because the Canadian government has done what most of them would do, in similar circumstances, to rescue citizens in trouble.

China in a Changing World

But Canadians will continue to be in the midst of trouble when they are outside of Canada. Tsunamis, hurricanes, volcanoes, earthquakes, and wars will continue; they will be victims of attacks; they will be arrested for crimes that are fully understood in North Bay; they will be arrested for crimes that will not be understood in North Bay; they will fall sick, and many will die. In the Caribbean, sun, sea, sex, and Seagram's will collect their usual toll.

Millions will travel and return with experiences that are life-changing, or simply experiences that provide for a better understanding of our phantasmagorical world. Each will be of great value to Canada as we seek to emphasize and demonstrate to the world that there is something unique under development in this northern land.

Suggesting to Canadians that they would be in danger should the government reach out to two Canadians imprisoned in China and bring them home is a denial of what Canada wants to be: a country that cares for its peoples wherever they are. This is fundamental to whatever Canadians are or will become. To argue that there is something else at play demonstrates that Canada's road to that future has become more difficult.

A final note reflecting the complexity for the Canadian government as it seeks an appropriate solution for this issue with China. There has been a spate of reports out of Washington during the past summer reflecting official American concerns with Canadian aluminum, dairy products, and lobster exports. Eventually, the American government imposed tariffs, at the time when the new trilateral free trade agreement had come into effect. Even Mary Poppins would see that it is not only China that is prepared to be nasty during a time of crisis.

Now the matter continues to drift as the government comes to grips with containing the effects of the COVID-19 pandemic and the reopening of the economy. In the meantime, relations with China are in a state of inaction and suspension. However, Kovrig and Spavor remain imprisoned without any expectation that anything will change. By not acting now with an available legal solution, the Canadian government may create a situation in which decisions by others could see Meng released from her sequestration and allowed to leave Canada, while at the same time Kovrig and Spavor would remain imprisoned in China.

14. A New World – Conclusions and an Agenda for the Future

> *In this new world, "leaders" have very little to do with leading. Instead, they avoid a world where there is great fluidity in the commonalities of space, time, environment, and a desire for a peaceful and secure future.*

In so many wrong ways, an aspect of today's discussions on the state of the world depends on the emergence of new "empires" or superpowers or new hegemonies. These are convenient escapes, if not tropes reflecting past disasters. Rather, it is the intensification of worldwide travel, the migration of peoples, global trade, and viruses that describes today's world. In this world, "leaders" have very little to do with leading. Instead, they avoid a world where there is great fluidity in the management of our commonalities of space, time, environment, and a desire for a peaceful and secure future.

They are the followers of the past with neither vision nor ability to understand the world that has been created as they move their bankrupt ideas around a board they do not understand. Not so many years ago, migration was a one-way affair with little to no expectation that a return "home," either physically or metaphorically, was possible. Equally, not so many years ago, a telephone conversation between Vancouver and the Punjab or Fujian was based more on hope than any expectation it would actually take place or an understandable conversation would occur.

China in a Changing World

Before COVID-19 interrupted our lives, over two billion people were taking to the skies for trips to other countries, and no trip to a far destination needed to be longer than a day. A telephone call to India or China is but an inconsequential interruption on a bike ride through the Canadian countryside. And for millions, an escape from the deadly daily dangers of war, onto neighbouring seas or across hostile bordering rivers or into jungles, is a risk worth taking.

The countries of the world have, crab-like, come to some measure of understanding that there is only one physical world and a sunrise in Shanghai is not much different than one in Halifax. The earth is one place and its physical well-being is the responsibility of all. Any expectation of it remaining as a place of comfort and personal well-being requires enormous international cooperation.

There is no less a need of worldwide cooperation for our political world if we are to continue into a future that beckons us from our confused today. In this new world, there is no need for "empires," "hegemonies," "domination," "containment," or policies based on "toughness" towards others. Rather, with the evident weaknesses of our recent "empires," there is an opportunity for the creation of a new world. In the main, the necessary institutions are already in place, having being created out of the ashes of the last world war and the slow promotion of cooperation by populations hungry for fewer dangers in their daily lives. And as was discussed in the opening pages of this book, the countries of the world in the middle of a global war could give attention to the need for the management of our common political affairs. There is a need for a renewal of that earlier wartime effort to ensure a more peaceful future. This could be a coalition of *United Democracies.*

Several decades ago, a character in an American satirical comic strip offered the most succinct description of our common problem in moving forward into a better world. Pogo, an opossum from the Okefenokee Swamp, summed up the world's problem in a memorial comment published on Earth Day in 1971: "We have met the enemy and he is us." That pithy aphorism was and remains central to our common effort for a better world, and it is one that leaders who "mislead" have disguised. Today it is easier to mislead than it is lead.

Democracy, along with its associated outriders of personal freedoms, liberty, and equality under law, has had a long and eventful history since the Greeks first gave thought to it some 2,500 years ago. In that context, it was the marketplace of ancient Athens that needed help, and the idea of cooperative commonality emerged. While "the involved peoples" of the time did not include everyone, it, more than other ideas of the period, survived the testing provided by worldwide experiences and challenges. Democracy's continuing widespread success provides the basis for all as a troubled future looms.

Winston Churchill, who had more experience than most with democracy (and autocracy and dictatorship), summed up democracy best when he said "democracy is the worst form of government except all the others that have been tried." And, echoing Pogo, Churchill also said "The best argument against democracy is a five-minute conversation with the average voter." Today, when polling plumbs the depths of the human condition and leaders rush to follow, we are fortunate that Churchill accurately established the beginning and end of our dilemma, if not our task. And if you are a person who assumes that Ecclesiastes got it right when he wrote some 2,300 or so years ago "there is nothing new under the sun," Marcus Cicero, a Roman and a favourite of Edward Gibbon (and no fan of empire),wrote more than two thousand years ago that

> A nation can survive its fools, and even the ambitious. But it cannot survive treason from within. For the traitor appears not a traitor—he speaks in the accents familiar to his victims, and he appeals to the baseness that lies deep in the hearts of all men. He rots the soul of a nation—he works secretly and unknown in the night to undermine the pillars of a city—he infects the body politic so that it can no longer resist. A murderer is less to be feared.

We can assume Cicero was not aware of the musing of President Trump in 2017 about the possibility of murder on Fifth Avenue in New York.

China in a Changing World

It is in the context of a new America under President Biden, an ascendant China, and a dithering and troublesome Russia that the opportunity for the involvement of Canada and tens of other like-minded countries could become manifest in developing and implementing a number of measures promoting the common interest. In some measure, it is not a time for new initiatives, but rather for the revalidation and expansion of existing or moribund initiatives and organizations. The inventory of such initiatives is a long one, but large changes for an increasingly phantasmagoric world require cooperation at a level beyond anything the world has seen since emerging from the wars of the mid-twentieth century. The need, today, is just as great and the opportunities for a new coalition of the willing is upon us. But there is a need for initiative and action now.

Ongoing debate in Canada around how to deal with the new China has degraded through confusion and indirection over the last few years, but could provide the starting point of a new dynamic in helping the world through many of its complex and increasing problems. Canada's inability to gain election to the UN Security Council in its last two efforts should be more worrisome to Canadians. It represents more than a "vanity project," and if there is any expectation that Canada can re-emerge as a voice of some importance in the world, then large initiatives need to be taken.

There is much more than "vanity" involved in doing so. Canada's continued economic well-being is dependent on a peaceful, cooperating world, and as is now evident, our physical health is contingent on this as well. The dark clouds of climate change will be felt more in a country as vast as Canada than in most, creating the imperative for cooperation on a global basis. Equally, we live next to a superpower that is undergoing serious renovation problems, and early indications are this will be a prolonged and troublesome period. Canada could be seen by the American warring factions both as an easy target of complaint or as a helpful fixer. Either way, this might be of help as the United States adjusts to a diminished role in the world.

It is in this confluence of factors that Canada's urge to play a larger role internationally must be considered. Yet, the examination of our collective entrails in an ongoing, inconclusive national debate is a luxury that a troubled world will not wait on. The problems are vast, but Canada's resources in people and money are equally vast. What is now needed is leadership that sees beyond the fog of St. John's, the rain in Victoria, and the melting ice in Resolute Bay, and helps establish coherency and direction for the only world we have and will ever have.

The agenda for a Canadian initiative on global matters is not difficult to establish. Positive steps in moderating conflict, improving cooperation, and creating change on a global basis can be achieved through consensus with a like-minded group. As a first step, and as the coronavirus fades, Canada could invite the world to a conference to begin a process that will lead to greater global unity, cooperation, and progress. This would be an enormous project involving the whole country and taking several years to achieve. But in a troubled world where preoccupation with oneself is normal, there is a need for an initiative or first step by a country with stature and experience. Canada could be that country.

A preliminary and by no means exclusive agenda for immediate action and for initiating this world conference would include some or all of the following:

Indigenous Peoples. The translation of the UN Declaration of the Rights of Indigenous Peoples from being a "declaration" to a legally binding set of obligations for all countries in their relationship with Indigenous peoples is needed. As the experience of Canada and many other countries has demonstrated, there is a need to provide greater international coherence and support for these largely forgotten and abused peoples with a higher level of pre-eminence in the management of global affairs. People are hidden by disappearing through the effects of imperialism, colonialism, and national policies, and action is required to counter and eliminate these effects. In doing so, the opening affirmations of the UN Charter can be expanded. The charter includes the statement: "We the peoples of the United Nations [. . .] reaffirm faith in fundamental human rights, in the dignity and worth of the human person, in the equal rights of men and women and of nations large and small." Indigenous peoples are rarely part of that reaffirmation.

Rules of War. The international rules on war and its frequent troublesome associates of internal wars and violence by national governments and non-state actors directed at civilians needs to be examined to give full effect to the obligations in the UN Charter. Again, the obligations of the charter have been ignored and abused by a wide variety of member states without concerted countering action.

Since the end of the Second World War, there have been numerous wars initiated by the Soviet Union/Russia, the United States, and a variety of other UN member countries. Some were sanctioned by decisions of the Security Council. Most were not, but were instead the initiative of member countries acting for reasons that were dubious, and often, in the end, failures. The loss of life across the spectrum of civilians and military personnel along with the destruction of countries has been enormous. In most cases there was little justification, even when the informal rules of "just war" theory were applied. There is also a need for an examination of the "self-defence" rules as they apply to the initiation of war by member countries of the United Nations.

Climate Change. A re-energization of the United Nations Framework Convention on Climate Change (UNFCCC) is needed. While some 189 countries are signatories of this convention, the United States has indicated that it will withdraw from the Paris Agreement aspects under the convention. This would be effective in November 2020, and whether it plays out during the election is unknown. But an early objective for Canada and others is to have the United States recommit to the Paris Agreement and return to a leadership role in the ongoing effort to mitigate the emission of greenhouse gases.

World Trade Organization. The United States has slowed (if not stopped) ongoing work under the World Trade Organization through various administrative measures. An early initiative is to ensure the re-engagement of the United States in the work of the WTO, see the WTO emerge as the global initiator of improvements to the world's trading system, and re-energize its work on an effective trade dispute mechanism.

Nuclear Weapons. Earlier global and bilateral initiatives created an environment where the development and use of nuclear weapons was circumscribed. These initiatives, including the Nuclear Non-Proliferation Treaty and United States–Soviet Union bilateral agreements reducing their respective numbers of nuclear weapons and associated delivery systems, are under suspension or considerable stress. In their time, these were highly successful and essential arrangements and a collective effort is needed to see their objectives revalidated, renewed, and expanded. This could begin with commitments by the United Kingdom and France to eliminate their nuclear weapons inventory, the establishment of commitments by all countries in Asia to commit to a joint non-first-use of nuclear weapons policy, and the start of a process that would lead to the elimination of nuclear weapons in the region. Such a process in Asia could lead to a similar initiative in the Middle East, and ultimately, one also involving the United States and Russia.

Asia-Pacific Trade. The United States, while initially involved in negotiations for the Trans-Pacific Partnership, signed on to the agreement in February 2016. However, President Trump withdrew the United States in January 2017. The other ten countries then negotiated a new trade agreement, the Comprehensive and Progressive Agreement for Trans-Pacific Partnership, which entered into force on December 30, 2018. An early initiative by Canada and others would be to have the United States join the new trade agreement, which includes most of the provisions of the earlier agreement. The effort should involve the inclusion of China.

UN Security Council. The United Nations and its vast family of associated specialized agencies celebrated its seventy-fifth anniversary in 2020. The essential work performed by the Security Council and General Assembly is in need of examination, reflection, and change. An early initiative by Canada and others would see to the formation of an assembly of international worthies to research and provide recommendations on changes that could update what was created seventy-five years ago. Key components of that work would be an effort to limit the authority of the five permanent members of the Security Council and their use of the veto, or broaden the number of permanent members along with the removal of the veto as a barrier to decision-making, and a majority voting system for decision-making.

UN Specialized Agencies. The fifteen specialized agencies of the United Nations all have authority under their mandates to examine and update their activities in a changing world. Most have done so and it can be expected that they will continue to do so in the years ahead. However, there is one in need of urgent attention in the context of recent and ongoing disasters. The World Health Organization (WHO) has undertaken an examination of its own policies and work related to the current COVID-19 pandemic, as well as earlier health emergencies. The announced work by the WHO so far suggests that the examination is specifically related to these pandemics and associated large diseases. There is also a need for a much broader examination of the WHO's mandate and activities. It would be appropriate for Canada and other members to promote this broader examination at the earliest possible date.

Laws of the Sea. The world's oceans are a major source of food. Nature has provided a bountiful menu of foods for millions of years. This food source is currently under stress and in danger of disappearing more than ever before. Indiscriminate harvesting practices by some countries, which are often called "vacuuming," continue and will only end with the elimination of a species.

To a limited extent, the Law of the Sea Convention has provided relief by extending national boundaries into the oceans and national controls over fishing. But these controls have also left vast areas of ocean *without* controls or protection from marauding fishing fleets. The oceans are also now recognized as an essential element in any successful global effort to deal with climate change. One aspect in that recognition should be efforts to provide international controls on the indiscriminate exploitation of marine life, including fish. Canada, which was a source of ideas and negotiation for the earlier Law of the Sea Convention, should initiate a worldwide effort to establish controls on oceanic fishing.

UNHCR. The United Nations High Commissioner for Refugees (UNHCR) has a long and difficult history, and there is no indication that its work will ease or lessen in the coming years. The issue of refugees is one of the most contentious issues handled within the context of the United Nations, and despite numerous efforts to update its mandate, the changes have not met the changing needs. Canada and other like-minded countries should promote a complete examination of the issues associated with refugees, including the conditions leading to their creation, intermediate care, and ultimate settlement.

Consular Affairs. Associated indirectly with refugees are the people who migrate and travel freely. Affluence, migration, increasingly scattered families, students studying abroad, the balancing of labour and skills, and the occasional need to sit on a sandy beach when northern climes are gripped by February all contribute to the two billion people who keep international airlines flying and ships cruising. As well, on a daily basis, the media reports international trials, tribulations, civil (and not so civil) wars, the hardback of government hands, and the dark side of an unpredictable natural environment. The media also keeps us informed of the vicissitudes that are encountered and the lack of local help.

This is the realm of consular affairs, or the official assistance that is provided by governments to citizens in foreign countries. It is an aspect of international relations that has not changed much since the days when the kings of Europe sat down in Vienna in 1815 to tidy up after Napoleon was sent to a small island in the south Atlantic. Today there is a 1963-era convention established on the matter, but it does little more than inform how governments can establish offices to help their citizens in trouble.

Arrest and detention, dual citizenship, child abductions, harsh prison conditions, evacuations, and prisoner transfers remain issues of considerable concern to Canadians. These conditions could form an initiative by the government to try and establish an international consensus to improve the responsibilities of governments when foreigners come calling. Equally important to the continued growth of international travel is the need fora collective effort to restore some measure of facilitation to the onerous procedures associated with visas, customs, and security measures. There is a need to change the current dynamic, where every foreign visitor is considered a threat, to one of welcome and appreciation.

China in a Changing World

International Communications. One of the world's great features today is the ease of communications within and between its far reaches. All "nowheres" are now "somewhere," and regardless of location, there is instantaneous real-time communication and the associated flow of data in every format. This is a relatively new phenomenon, driven by national and commercial developments and involving three large technologies. The first is the Internet, developed largely by the United States Department of Defense in the 1960s, which provided for time-sharing of computers. The expansion of this basic communications technology from the needs of the military to the worlds of government, business, academia, institutions, and individuals has reshaped and enhanced all aspects of life. The associated World Wide Web, appearing in 1989, provides everyone with an overwhelming and interconnected abundance of information. The two thousand or so communication satellites in geostationary orbit round out a system that a few years ago was only found in works of science fiction.

The value of this system grows exponentially with its utilization in medicine, education, business, culture, and entertainment. Even in the troubled days of COVID-19, the importance of the system is proven daily in assessments of the spread of the virus, the sharing of new treatments, and the coordination of research for new vaccines.

Beyond criminal misuses of the Internet, there is growing evidence that governments are misusing the system as well. Here, the evidence is still emerging, but it is clear that this misuse represents a serious development in international relations and one requiring collective action by the international system. The popularization of the term "fake news" by the American president, probably based on his own activities and personal inclinations, provides a graphic illustration of how governments are misusing this relatively new and immensely valuable communications tool.

This vast communications system is without significant measure of governance or norms of behaviour by users. It is left to the world of technology and several immensely wealthy individuals to provide some measure of normative behaviour, and clearly that is insufficient when the actions of governments are involved. An early element for collective international action would be to investigate this area of international activity and try to establish normative rules of behaviour.

As this collection of issues demonstrates, there is no shortage of items that could occupy an international conference. However, for Canada to lead and/or participate in such an initiative, there is an immediate need for a revitalization of its foreign service. The service has been troubled with the lack of meaningful activities and associated resources for some time. Today it is a pale shadow of when initiatives were undertaken after 1945 and even throughout the 1970s and 1980s. Even more damaging was a willingness by governments to ignore the need for expertise as an essential element in their international activities. The author, in spite of a vested interest, pleads for such a renewal. The plea is made not only in the context of existing global requirements but also for the identification of knowledgeable and experienced experts to take on the complex tasks of giving appropriate form and substance to the solutions needed in a changing and troubled world.

About the author

Gar Pardy retired from the Canadian foreign service almost twenty years ago, after travelling the world since 1957 when he left Gander, Newfoundland, for a life in Labrador, Frobisher Bay, Ottawa, India, Kenya, the United States, and Central America. In his travels, his life intersected with that of Indira Gandhi, Mohammed Zahir Shah, Jomo Kenyatta, Idi Amin, Jimmy Carter, Ronald Reagan, George Bush, Bobby Inman, Robert Gates, John McLaughlin, Manuel Noriega, Oscar Arias, Violeta Chamorro, brothers Daniel and Humberto Ortega, Stanley Faulder, Nguyen Tai Heap, James Lockyer, Monia Mazigh, Maher Arar, Omar Khadr, Dennis Edney, Lorne Waldman, Marlys Edwardh, and Sandra Babcock.

At various times, Mr. Pardy's responsibilities and travels involved China and many of the countries discussed in this paper. He lives in Ottawa, and can be contacted at garp@rogers.com

Other writings by the author

- *Consular and Diplomatic Protection in the Age of Terrorism: Filling the Gaps* by Gar Pardy in **The Human Rights of Anti-terrorism,** edited by Nicole LaViolette and Craig Forcese, Irwin Law, Toronto, 2008
- **Shared Vision or Myopia: The Politics of Perimeter Security and Economic Competitiveness with the United States** by Gar Pardy, Centre for Policy Alternatives, 2011
- *The Long Way Home: The Saga of Omar Khadr* by Gar Pardy in **Omar Khadr, Oh Canada,** edited by Janice Williamson, McGill – Queen's University Press, Montreal, 2012
- **Afterwords from a Foreign Service Odyssey** by Gar Pardy, Friesen Press, Victoria, 2015

- **Canadians Abroad – A Policy and Legislative Agenda** by Gar Pardy, Rideau Institute, Ottawa, 2016
- **Political Violence and Kidnapped Canadians** by Gar Pardy, 2018

Gar Pardy has also published columns and articles in the *Ottawa Citizen*, the *Embassy* and *Hill Times*, *The Globe and Mail*, *the Kingston Whig Standard*, the *Edmonton Journal*, the *National Post*, the *Times Colonist, bout de papier, Diplomat and International Trade, iPolitics, Prism Magazine,* and others. Interviews with Pardy have been aired by the CBC, CTV, Global, and CPAC.

www.ingramcontent.com/pod-product-compliance
Lightning Source LLC
Chambersburg PA
CBHW070800040426
42333CB00060B/1347